The Academy of Golf at PGA National

The Complete Golf Manual

THIS IS A CARLTON BOOK

This edition published in 2001

10 9 8 7 6 5 4 3 2 1

A CIP catalogue reference for this book is available from the British Library.

ISBN 1-84222-254-6

Printed in Singapore

Acknowledgements

The authors would like to thank Kathryn Maloney who served as Project Manager. Kathryn is an LPGA Teaching Professional at Ironhorse Country Club in West Palm Beach, FL, and a freelance writer.

Photographs
All photographs by Marc Feldman with the exception of the following photographs on pages 89 (top), 103, 104 and 107, which were taken by Kathryn Maloney. The photographs on pages 181–184, 186 and 188 are produced courtesy of Allsport (Jon Ferrey).

Note: for convenience of presentation, we have presented the material in this book for right-handed golfers. Obviously, the mechanics of the golf swing will apply to all golfers.

The Academy of Golf at PGA National

The Complete Golf Manual

MIKE ADAMS & T.J. TOMASI
WITH KATHRYN MALONEY

Contents

10
LA COSTA
450 yds.
PAR 4

Introduction

Golf is listed in the dictionary as a game played by striking a small, resilient ball with clubs into a series of holes with natural and artificial obstacles irregularly interposed. It involves striking a ball the fewest number of times possible, over a vast expanse of territory, varying terrain and in changing weather conditions. In no other sport is the disparity between the size of the playing field and the goal (the cup) so large.

Golf is a game that is different from other sports in that it does not require an exceptional physique: you need not be seven feet tall, weigh 200 pounds, or be able to run 100 yards in less than ten seconds. You can excel at golf even if you aren't blessed with the natural attributes that are essential in many other sports. A golfer with a good short game is a match for anyone even if he doesn't drive the ball a mile. It is part of the fascination and frustration of the game that a three-foot putt and a three-hundred yard drive are of equal value on your score card.

In all sports where you have an opponent, your actions are a response to someone else's performance. What they do dramatically affects what you do. A baseball pitcher's choice of a curve ball versus a fast pitch determines the batter's behavior; the server in tennis dictates the response of the competitor on the other side of the net.

However, in golf, everything is self initiated because, by the rules of the game, the ball does not move unless you act on it. What you do to that ball depends solely on your own capabilities laced with a little luck. You have no coach and no team-mates to offer assistance or to blame when things go wrong. All the decisions and actions are your sole responsibility and it is this matrix of self-reliance that gives the game its wonderful character. During a round of golf the golf swing itself gets the most focus, but there is plenty of time for doing other things. In a four-and-a-half hour round where you took 90 swings (the average swing takes about 1.5 seconds), you would spend approximately two minutes and twenty-five seconds actually swinging the club. That leaves about four hours and twenty-seven minutes to relax and enjoy the company of your companions and the beauty of your playing field.

It won't ever be perfect

In golf, we should strive for perfection but never expect it. After all, golf is a target game, and the nature of targets is they can be, and often are, missed. In a game requiring such precision and accuracy, even a slight alteration of your swing can have significant effects on your ball flight. If you contact the ball just a quarter of an inch off of the sweet spot it can result in a loss of 30 yards. Thus it is wise to remember that expecting flawless performance in a game with such a small margin for error is asking for frustration.

Even though you can't attain perfection, it is true that the more sound your swing mechanics are, the more you will be rewarded with golf shots that go where you want them to. Thus it makes sense for you to develop a blueprint for your golf swing that is technically correct. This will allow you to play better golf with more consistency.

Develop a blueprint

The problem is that most golfers don't take the time to construct and follow a blueprint for building their golf swing because they are too busy looking for quick remedies. They want to do it the "easy way" with a tip that instantly makes the ball fly long and straight and they end up putting a band aid on their swing that works one day, and is gone the next.

We believe that you will play better golf if you follow our step-wise learning procedure which is designed to allow you to build a blueprint of your golf swing based on the time-tested fundamentals of what constitutes good golf.

The learning procedure

How can you learn to play better golf? Science shows us that an effective way to learn a skill like the golf swing is to divide it into manageable pieces and then to learn them one at a time. The procedure goes like this:

- First, you pick a perfect example of what you want to be able to do. It could be Pete Sampras's serve in tennis, or Ronaldo's shooting in soccer or Jack Nicklaus's grip in golf.
- Then once you have studied that model, you attempt to match it using a trial and correction procedure where your attempts bring you closer and closer to the prototype.
- Once you can match the prototype perfectly, the next step is to repeat the procedure again and again until it becomes a habit, i.e. you can do it automatically. In our example of learning the grip, you can place your hands on the club perfectly without even thinking about it. Chuck Hogan, an advisor to many tour players and an expert on how golfers learn the game, estimates that it takes at least 60 repetitions for 21 days in a row to produce a motor habit.

Whatever the exact number, there have been many professional golfers, including Greg Norman and Larry Nelson, who built their swing piece by piece using an instructional book as their model guide.

What's in the book

In the following chapters you will learn how to play better golf using this step-wise, piece-by-piece approach.

- **Chapters One and Two** present the building blocks of the swing, the pre-shot routine and the pre-swing mechanics, including the grip, stance, posture, aim and alignment. These set the stage for the sequential motion of your swing before the club is even set in motion.

Sometimes you have to look at the arrows rather than the archer, so to aid you in the selection of your clubs, we review some essentials of golf equipment so that you can make an informed decision about what is right for you.

- **Chapters Three to Five** describe the golf swing sequence, focusing in detail on the four key parts: the backswing, downswing, the position at impact and the follow through.

In support of the full swing instruction, special sections are provided that focus in depth on how to hit the driver, the long irons and fairway woods, the mid and short irons as well as the technique of drawing and fading the ball.

And in keeping with our belief that you can learn your own golf swing by copying the swings of others, some frame-by-frame annotated swing sequences of expert players are provided to serve as prototypes from which you can model your own golf swing.

- **Chapters Six and Seven** cover the specialty shots you need to know out on the golf course. These are the shots that call for some imagination as well as specific technical adjustments to your stance and swing. The special shots section includes advice on how to keep the ball under a tree limb, how and when to run the ball to the flag, how to handle bad lies and what to do when the ball is above your feet or perched on the side of a hill well below your feet.
- **Chapters Eight to Eleven** focus on the short game. Since 65 percent of the strokes you take are from 100 yards and in, pitching, putting, chipping and sand play make up an important segment of your blueprint for golf.
- **Chapters Twelve to Eighteen** deal with the actual playing of the game: how you think your way around a golf course, where to position your ball, what kind of shot to play based on your evaluations of the conditions (weather, pin position, lie etc.) and the circumstances of play (match or medal). Of equal importance to good course management is good self-management, so a section dealing with the inner game of golf has been included.

It's been said that practice makes perfect but in reality only perfect practice makes perfect so we've outlined for you some perfectly designed practice routines that will speed you on your way to playing better golf.

Summary

As you can see from this brief overview, the purpose of this book is quite simply to help you play better golf. In the final analysis, your development depends on your ability to take control of your own learning process. Improvement in golf is an evolution—a gradual, continuous process. Our job is to get you started in the right direction.

The authors

T.J. Tomasi is the Director of the Players School at the Academy of Golf at PGA National. With over 20 years of teaching experience, he is also one of the most widely published golf instructors in the world and has served as the instructional editor of *Golf Illustrated* and *Golfing* magazines. Dr. Tomasi has a Ph.D. in Education.

The Academy of Golf at PGA National at Palm Beach Gardens, Florida, is one of America's most comprehensive golf schools. The Academy of Golf affords the student access to the top golf instructors, superb teaching facilities and the latest technology.

Mike Adams, a former PGA touring professional, is Director of the PGA's National Academy of Golf at Palm Beach Gardens, Florida. Known throughout the world as the "Swing Doctor," Adams has a keen eye for detecting swing flaws, and an impressive track record for correcting them. He is one of America's most sought-after golf teachers, teaching more than 3,000 individual lessons each year. Hollywood celebrities who have Adams to thank for their golf skills include Jack Nicholson, Michael Douglas, Willie Nelson and Tom Landry. President Bill Clinton worked with the "Swing Doctor" when he visited the PGA National in March 1995, and former President Gerald Ford was another pupil of Mike Adams. Recently voted one of America's 100 Best Golf Teachers by *Golf Magazine*, Adams writes instruction articles for *Golf Magazine*, *Golf Digest* and *Golfing*.

Chapter one

Equipment

In the past decade, through sophisticated computers linked with video cameras and other measuring devices, the effects of club specifications on the flight of the golf ball, (for example, loft and lie), have been well documented. The results are clear: learning to swing the golf club correctly is directly dependent on having the correct golf club to swing.

To maximize your performance in golf you should fit your golf clubs and your golf ball to your own personal characteristics, such as swing speed, strength, and body type. For example, if you're using a club shaft that is too stiff for you, you'll leave your weight on your right side during the downswing in order to get the ball up in the air. Thus, subconsciously, you have introduced an error into your golf swing to compensate for a misfit club specification.

Equipment innovations include the long-shafter putter, which has helped Bruce Lietzke.

Club specification

The club specifications that have the most effect on your swing and are thus of primary importance to you as a golfer are as follows: the lie angle, club length, shaft stiffness, loft angle and weight.

Lie angle

The lie angle is measured by a line from the center line of the shaft to the ground when the club is soled correctly. There are two aspects to lie angle:

- The lie angle that's created as the club sits unmoving on the ground as described above.
- The effective lie angle which changes as you swing when the shaft bows downward, causing the toe of the club to get closer to the ground. This is the dynamic aspect of lie and also the reason why the irons are fitted with the toe slightly up in the air.

Note: If your lie angle is off, your divots may tell you. If the divot is toe deep, your clubs are too flat; if it's heel deep, your clubs are too upright.

The wrong lie

Lie angle that is too upright at impact causes your ball to go to the left of target. If it's too flat (toe down), your ball goes to the right of the target, assuming that, in both instances, you have aimed correctly.

With mis-fit lie angles, it is very easy to groove a swing error. If you make good golf swings and the ball consistently flies to the right of the target, it won't be long before you introduce an over-the-top move to pull the ball back to target. However, if your ball flies to the left, you will delay your hands to block the ball back to the target.

The important point here is that you may have a static lie angle which appears to fit you, but as soon as the club starts in motion, the lie angle becomes a function of how fast you swing, how strong you are, and your hand action through impact. There is only one way to tell how your individual characteristics will affect the static specification of lie and that is to experiment with it while you swing. This is part of a good fitting process and any fitter worth his salt will have the proper tools to determine in-swing lie angle.

Flat and *upright clubs*

The club is referred to as being "flat" when the toe moves downward toward the ground; when it moves toward the sky it's called "upright." In order to get a square club face at impact, you may have to adjust the lie of your club at address. You can have your clubs either bent flat or upright in a lie machine, depending on your body and swing characteristics.

When you lengthen a club, the club head gets more upright (toe up) as you stand farther away. As you shorten the club, you stand over the ball more and the toe flattens. The rule of thumb is that adding a half an inch of length, makes the club more upright by about one degree.

1 The correct lie angle aims the club face down the target line.
2 When the lie angle is too upright, the club aims left.
3 Too flat a lie aims the club face right.

Club length

All other things being equal, the longer the shaft, the further you'll hit the ball. However, there is a trade off because it's harder to make square contact using the longer shaft and you can lose distance if the contact isn't on the sweet spot of the club.

Besides feel, you can use impact tape or chalk to determine the centeredness of hit for each swing. To find out which length is right for you, tape each club face and try out three different shaft lengths, hitting 10 shots with each length on two separate occasions. As soon as your percentage of off-center hits is greater than 30 percent, the shaft is too long.

Extra-long *drivers*

Traditionally drivers have been about 43 inches with about 11 degrees of loft. Today's driver shafts are getting longer thanks to the new, much lighter shaft materials being used. Rocky Thompson's 52-inch driver has transformed him from being a relatively short hitter into one of the longest hitters on the Senior Tour. Studies show that if you lengthen your driver by two inches you can add about four miles per hour to your swing speed, about a 12-yard increase in distance. One caveat: it's tricky simply extending the length of your current driver, because when you change one specification, it changes the others.

Club specification *continued*

Club length *continued*

You will have balance problems when your club length is wrong because club length affects your posture, and it is proper posture that promotes good balance while you swing. If your clubs are too long you will compensate by standing too upright, and in doing so, your weight transfers back on your heels and your arms can't hang freely. Conversely, when your clubs are too short, you bend over too much, forcing your weight onto your toes.

1 Clubs that are too long cause a rigid, erect posture.

2 Clubs that are not long enough will force excessive tilting of the spine.

Shaft stiffness

Where and how much your shaft flexes while you swing determines your club face position at impact. If the shaft is too whippy, it's hard to square your club face at impact, whereas if it's too stiff, it won't bend enough, leaving your club face open through the hitting zone.

Generally, most golfers use too stiff a shaft. Your goal should be to swing the most flexible shaft you can handle without the ball flying all over the place. If your shots are going low and to the right, your shafts are too stiff. If your shot pattern is unpredictable, i.e. some to the left and some to the right, then your shaft is probably too flexible.

Loft angle

The non-technical description of loft is how much your club face looks at the sky, and it has a major effect on the height and trajectory of your golf shot. It's difficult to make a well-balanced, well-timed energy transfer with too little loft on your clubs because you'll subconsciously make adjustments in your swing to get the ball in the air. However, too much loft costs you distance and encourages over-swinging.

Adjusting loft from the normal is known as strengthening or weakening. You will strengthen your pitching wedge by changing it from 56 degrees of loft to 54 degrees and consequently you'll hit the ball lower and a little bit longer. Weakening works in reverse and is used to raise the trajectory.

Weight

The total weight of the golf club is the actual scale weight or "dead weight"; for example, 13 ounces. It is important because if your club is too heavy for you, your swing gets out of control, whereas if it's too light, you can't feel the shaft.

The swing weight is the relationship between the length of the club and the amount of weight in the head. How the weight is distributed determines the "feel" of the club head. Swing weight should be the same for all your clubs to promote overall feel, but the scale weight differs for each, with your sand wedge being the heaviest.

Although there are other specifications, lie, loft, length, flex and weight are the "big five" of club specifications and if you get them right, you'll have a set of clubs that rewards balance, timing and the energy transfer necessary to get the ball to target.

Length, lie and loft

Note: Standard isn't always standard.

	length in inches	lie in degrees	loft in degrees
Woods			
Driver	43+	55	11 to 13
3	42	57	13 to 16
4	41	58	16 to 19
5	40	59	19 to 21
7	40	60	25 to 27
Irons			
1	39.5	58	17
2	39	59	21
3	38.5	60	25
4	38	61	29
5	37.5	62	33
6	37	63	37
7	36.5	64	41
8	36	65	45
9	35.5	66	49
PW	35	67	53
SW	35	67	57

Overall, the best way to determine which clubs are right for you is the "hit 'em and fit 'em" technique; in other words, be fitted by an expert while you are actually swinging the club.

Weight *control*

The overall weight of your club is as important as how that weight is distributed (swing weight). This is because clubs that are too heavy for you can cause swing faults. One way to tell is to monitor your last five rounds of golf to see if the clubs become "heavier" as the round progresses. If you're swinging the correct weight clubs, you shouldn't notice much of a difference from your first swing to your last.

Another sign of too-heavy clubs is an overswing where you lose control at the top of your swing as your club head dips well below your shoulders pointing to the right of the target. If you can see the club head out of the corner of your eye, have your clubs checked.

It's nice to inherit a set of clubs but they may not be right for you, especially if they're men's clubs and you're a woman or a junior golfer. You should also "try before you buy," no matter how attractive the price.

Club specification *continued*

Game improvement

Perimeter weighting is a process in which a cavity is created by taking weight from the back of the club and distributing it around the perimeter. This reduces twisting when you contact the ball off the sweet spot, minimizing both the distance and directional loss that accompany off-center hits with traditional forged clubs.

This is the secret of over-size club heads, both woods and irons, and it's the new materials, such as titanium, that make perimeter weighting more effective. The lightness and strength of titanium allow club manufacturers greater versatility in shifting the weight around the club head and increasing its overall size. A typical stainless steel head weighs about seven ounces (200 grams) while the titanium version is a mere four ounces (120 grams). The club maker using titanium has three ounces (80 additional grams) to make game improvement changes, such as super-sized club heads and extreme perimeter weighting, that keep your drives flying straight.

Above left: a perimeter weighted, oversize head for maximum game improvement. Center: a standard size "forgiveness", perimeter weighted head. Right: a traditional forge head offering the advanced golfer a softer feel and feedback about off-center hits.

What's in *the bag*

A sound golf swing and well-fitted equipment are a powerful combination for maximizing your potential as a golfer. You can take this one step farther by matching your equipment to the specific characteristics of each golf course and the conditions of the day.

Our advice is that you assemble some specialized clubs and then rotate them in your bag as supplements to your core set so that your equipment is tailored to the job at hand. Strong additions to your arsenal might be wedges with varying degrees of bounce and loft, a five, six and seven wood, a long-shafted driver, a chipper and a cavity-back driving iron with an over-sized head, and an assortment of putters.

Swing speed and club specifications

Club speed is the velocity of the club head as it passes through the four inches just preceding the ball. For every one mile an hour that you increase your club head speed, you can generate about three more yards in distance.

Swing speed	Shaft flex	Flex point	Golfer categories
very slow < 60 mph	very flex very soft	lowest	senior women and super senior men
slow 60 to 80 mph	flexible, "A" or senior shaft	low	amateur women and senior men
medium 81—94 mph	regular to firm	middle	amateur men and seniors/women pros
fast 95—110 mph	firm to stiff	high	long hitting amateur, golf pros, very long women tour pros
very fast 110 +	stiff to extra stiff	highest	very long tour pros, long drive competitors

Note: Companies vary in their shaft flex designations.

Which ball?

Golf balls are available with basically two types of covers: Surlyn and Balata. The average golfer likes the durability of Surlyn whereas the top players favor Balata because of high spin rates that allow them to "work" the ball, i.e. curve it left and right, hit it high and low.

Ball construction

Two-piece balls have solid interiors and an outer cover, while three-piece balls have a liquid core surrounded by a rubber winding, covered by either a Surlyn or Balata outer shell. If you are looking for distance, use a two-piece ball with a low spin rate; it will also minimize slicing and hooking by reducing side spin.

With the introduction of Lithium Surlyn, a softer cover which gives you more feel and a high spin rate, the playing characteristics between three- and two-piece have narrowed considerably. Increasingly, golfers are choosing their balls on the basis of spin rate, i.e. how fast the ball spins around its axis.

- For control and maneuverability, choose a ball with a high spin rate and a soft cover.
- For maximum distance and a durable golf ball that flies higher and gets more roll, you should opt for the two-piece ball with a low spin rate.
- For a distance and control blend, opt for a combination: a moderate spin rate with a durable cover.

Nowadays you can actually fit the components of the ball to your swing and to the type of shots that you want to make. It's like a ski racer matching a ski wax to the snow conditions.

Dimple arrangement

Back in the early days of the game, golfers learned that if you scuffed up the ball, it had a tendency to fly better and that was the beginning of the quest for the perfect dimple pattern.

The key elements are the depth, diameter, number and shape of the dimples. Manufacturers create different trajectories, distance, and spin by adjusting the dimple pattern and it's up to you to match your skill level to the appropriate pattern.

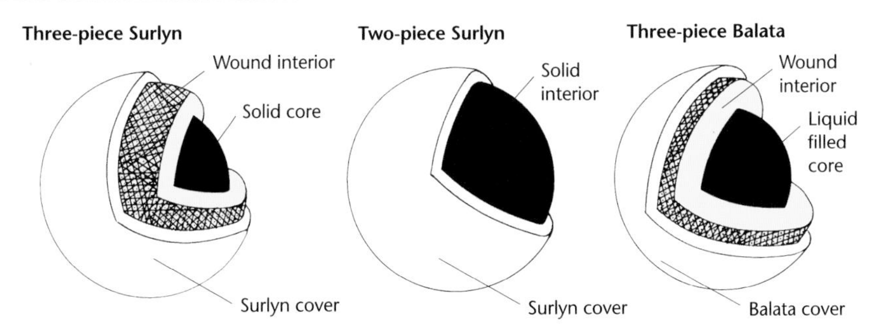

Performance
Specs

Ball choice spin rate

Workability	
3-piece Balata (intentional curving)	*high*
Decrease slices and hooks	
2-piece Surlyn	*low*
Distance	
2-piece Surlyn	*low*
Best around the greens	
3-piece Balata	*high*
Trajectory	
High = Surlyn	*high to medium*
Low = Balata	*low*
Combine distance and direction	
3-piece Surlyn	*medium to high*

Note: Lithium Surlyn combination covers can produce very high spin rates.

Golf balls may look very similar but their construction and inner make-up can be very different indeed. Pictured here are a two-piece Surlyn ball (left), a three-piece Balata ball (center) and a two-piece Surlyn wound ball (right). You'll improve your score when the ball you choose matches well with your swing and the conditions of play.

Driver
tip

Shortening the shaft in your driver for increased accuracy is a good idea if you face a "tight course." The amount you sacrifice in distance should be a fair exchange for staying out of the woods and hazards. Jack Nicklaus played much of his career with a less than standard length driver and in many situations he chose his three wood off the tee.

Equipment selection

Golf courses can be categorized broadly as:

1. "Driver courses"
2. "Second shot courses"
3. "Third shot courses"

Driver courses

A "driver course", which is characterized by narrow fairways and hazards bordering landing areas, demands accuracy off the tee. The greens are often large and receptive if you meet the driving conditions.

Examples of driver courses

Courses such as Royal Lytham in England, and Carnoustie in Scotland, Tryall in Jamaica, and Oak Hill in New York are good examples.

Along the seaside, or in the absence of a watering system, you'll often find the wind-swept fairways dry and firm. These "fast" conditions are a good opportunity to give your driver a rest for the day. Your three wood will get you plenty of distance off the tee, and since it produces shots that fly higher and land softer, your ball won't run off the fairway and into the rough as it might with the "hot" rolling driver.

The challenge of a driver course is to hit as many fairways as possible. A one iron, while difficult to hit from the fairway, can be an asset off the tee. With the objective being accuracy, you can count on your "driving iron" to go reasonably straight even if you mis-hit it.

Another consideration is the height of the rough. Low rough that's not much of a penalty means that the course is wider than it looks so keep your driver in the line up. Alternatively, high rough can make the three wood or an iron off the tee the wise choice, even if the fairway is relatively wide.

Second shot courses

Greens that are tough to hit usually have generous fairways but the "second shot course" does demand that you hit your tee shot a long distance. If this is not already one of your strengths, let the longer shafted driver help you cover more ground. The longer shaft, about 44 to 48 inches, produces a wider arc, faster club head speed and increased distance but its length can make it difficult to square the face at impact so make sure that you can handle the big stick.

Examples of second shot courses

Pebble Beach in California, Firestone in Ohio, St. Andrews in Scotland and many of Jack Nicklaus's designs typify the second shot concept.

Before you strap on your spikes, check the conditions. For example, wet conditions make even the average-length course play long. The "slow" course provides little roll for tee shots and that means longer approach shots. If you're a good player (single digit), select a driver with a sole plate designed to make it easier to hit off the fairway in case you need it. And no matter what your skill level, be sure to add your strong three wood for the longer carries.

The second shot course has generous landing areas for your tee shots but be prepared for plenty of pitches, chips and bunker shots because the greens are typically small or obliquely angled and always well guarded by hazards. You may want to put a "chipper" in your bag because the weighting system for this specialty club is designed to roll the ball accurately to the hole from just off the green.

Two putters can help, if you're playing a "second shot course" where you're likely to miss a lot of greens: your regular putter for the lag putts and the long putter anchored at the top of your chest for the "knee knockers." Because of its pendulum motion, the long putter works well from short distances but the longer your backswing the more inaccurate it becomes, so unless you practice regularly, it's tough to judge the lag putts.

Third shot courses

The "third shot course" is typified by large, fast greens with severe undulations and slopes. The battle really begins once your ball is on the green. Your putting skills need to be polished and your putting strategy must begin with your approach shot because although the greens are large, you must play to specific locations, positioning your ball on the correct tier and below the hole so that you're putting uphill. Be exact about your yardage—missing your area on a "third shot" course can mean the difference between a 70-foot putt and a ten-footer. Some architects even build "collection areas" where the ball can be funneled off the green and onto the fringe.

Examples of third shot courses

Augusta National in Georgia, Oakmont in Pennsylvania and The East Course at The Broadmoor in Colorado are good examples.

One or two *putters?*

When you're scheduled to play a third shot course where green speed varies, your putting touch will determine your success so once again consider carrying two putters. Always use a light-weight putter for the lightning fast, down-grain, downslope attempts, and a heavy putter that will help to get the ball rolling against the grain and up the steep slopes. And don't rule out the long putter as described (left).

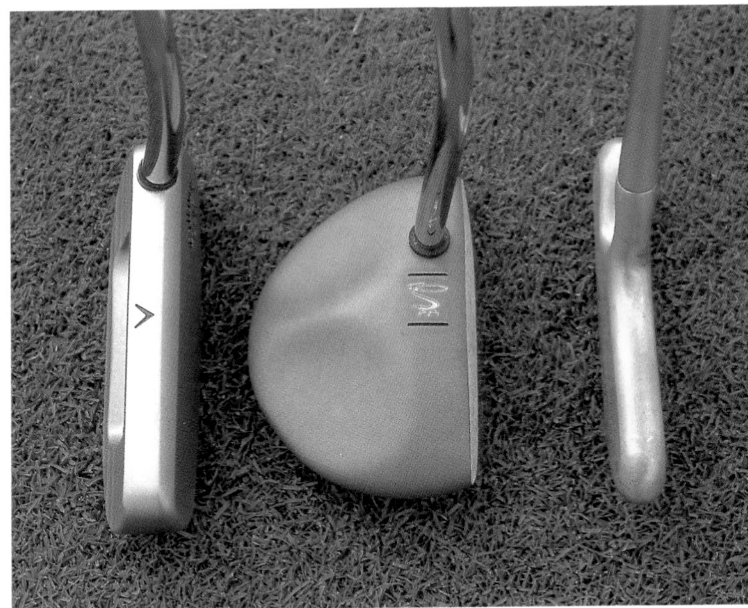

A box head putter (left) offers forgiveness for off-center hits; the weight of a mallet head (center) helps get the ball to the hole on slow greens; a blade putter (right) produces better feel on fast greens.

Utility woods and wedges

The woods

The utility woods are fast replacing the long irons; there's no mistaking the advances in design making them easy to hit from a wide range of lies. On a tight course with narrow fairways guarded by rough, be sure to pack your five, six and/or seven woods. If you are playing a course with a lot of well-guarded par threes and you hit your long irons very low, use a utility wood to get the required distance and trajectory. And when you need a high shot that holds the green, there's nothing better than a seven wood. It goes about the same distance as your three iron but much higher.

The wedges

You can save strokes if you choose your wedges correctly. The performance of a wedge is significantly influenced by the design of the sole. The term "bounce" is used to describe the effectiveness of the club in deflecting (bouncing) off a surface of grass, sand or dirt at impact. The greater the bounce, the farther it extends below the leading edge, preventing your club head from digging into the ground.

A pitching wedge with 50 degrees of loft and about four degrees of bounce, works pretty well from tight lies as well as from the fairway. The average sand wedge has around 56 degrees loft with 11 degrees bounce to prevent the leading edge from digging into the sand. It works well in soft sand and around the greens in normal green-side rough.

The lob wedge has between 60 and 64 degrees of loft with a small amount of bounce. It works well from wet, hard sand or hardpan and, with its loft, it can get the ball up in a hurry so that it lands softly from a tight lie. Its maximum range is usually about 70 yards.

Let the conditions of play dictate the amount of bounce you select when choosing a wedge.
Left: 57° with 11° of bounce (large bounce).
Center: 53° with 9° of bounce (small bounce).
Right: 61° with 3° lob (zero bounce).

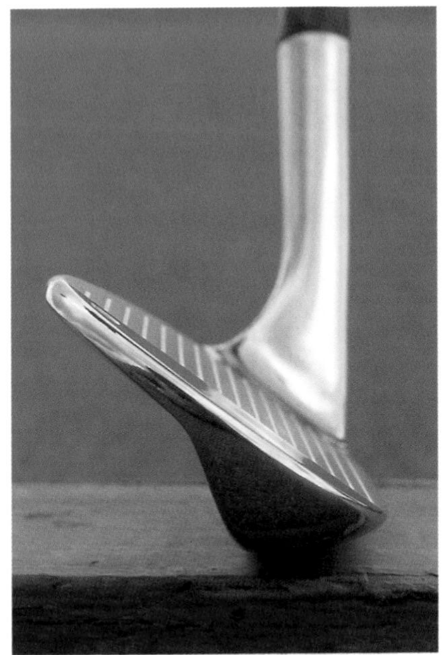

When correctly soled, only the bounce of the sand wedge touches the ground.

On a "second shot course," in windy conditions or if you generally miss lots of greens, you should definitely consider an extra wedge—or two. In addition to your pitching and sand wedges, the third wedge (often called the lob wedge), is a versatile high-lofted (60-degree) club which helps you to pitch the ball high and soft from all sorts of lies.

A fourth wedge is not unheard of, especially if you face short pitches from tight, closely mowed fairways where you need a wedge with little bounce. It can also be useful as a "gap" wedge if you have a large gap between the distances you hit your pitching and sand wedges. Thus if you hit your pitching wedge 120 yards and your full sand wedge only 90 yards, the difference (30 yards) is too great, forcing you to either let up too much on your pitching wedge or swing too hard at your sand wedge. In our example you would adjust the loft and shaft length on your wedge to hit the ball about 110 yards.

If your bag cannot accommodate a fourth wedge, another solution to the "gap" problem is to lengthen the shaft of your sand wedge and/or decrease its loft. This increases its overall distance for a full swing and then, by simply gripping it down an inch or two, you can hit it about 10 yards shorter when you need to.

In the bunker you can save some strokes by matching your sand wedge system to the texture of the sand. When it is soft and fluffy, use a wedge with a large flange and a lot of bounce. When the sand is hard, wet or crusty, select a wedge with minimal flange and bounce.

Core set plus strategy set

The Rules of Golf limit you to 14 clubs so when you are deciding which ones to include in your bag, you may have to make some difficult trade offs. To stay within the 14 club limit carry the five, six, seven, eight and nine irons, pitching wedge, sand wedge, putter and driver or three wood in your core set. Then add your strategy clubs, depending on the course, the weather, how you feel and how well you are swinging.

Bermuda *grass*

In thick Bermuda rough, a ball that is nestled down can be extracted only with a firm blow. If you play a course with a lot of Bermuda, select the sand and lob wedges with shorter, more flexible shafts so that you can make a long, accelerating swing that will blast your ball out of the rough and still allow it to land softly on the green.

Chapter two

The set up

Steve Elkington's picture-perfect golf swing is founded on his precise and fundamentally sound set up. Note especially the look of relaxed readiness.

The term "set up" is a good one because that's just what this portion of your pre-shot routine does: it sets up your whole swing. Now you may not have the athletic talent of a tour player once the swing starts (few people do) but every golfer has the ability to set up like an expert so there are no excuses when it comes to getting this part of your swing perfect.

No matter what method they teach, you won't get much argument from golf instructors when you say that the correct set up is essential to a good golf swing. The set up writes the script for the performance of your golf swing. How you position your body in relation to your golf club, the ball and the target has a major effect on the quality of your golf shot. A proper set up encourages proper motion throughout your swing; an improper set up encourages swing flaws. We estimate that over 90 percent of all swing errors are caused by an improper set up. For example, if you mis-aim too far to the right of the target (a common set up error made by over 80 percent of golfers), you must either flip your hands over at impact in order to hook the ball back to the target or you have to rotate your chest and pull the ball back to target. Either way you have introduced one error to compensate for another and you cannot play your best golf with a patchwork quilt of errors that can unravel at the least provocation.

The grip

The initial fundamental for a good set up is a correct grip. The function of the grip is to establish and maintain control of the club face, to allow the proper hinging of the wrists and to create a connection between your body and the club.

Your left-hand grip

1 Hold the club in front of you in your right hand at a 45-degree angle.

2 Place the side of the shaft across the base of the fingers of your left hand. The club will rest between the two creases (the Palmer creases) so that when you close your hand, it will be anchored under the heel pad of the left hand, thereby giving you control of the club without inducing any tension. This will also allow your wrist to hinge properly throughout the golf swing.

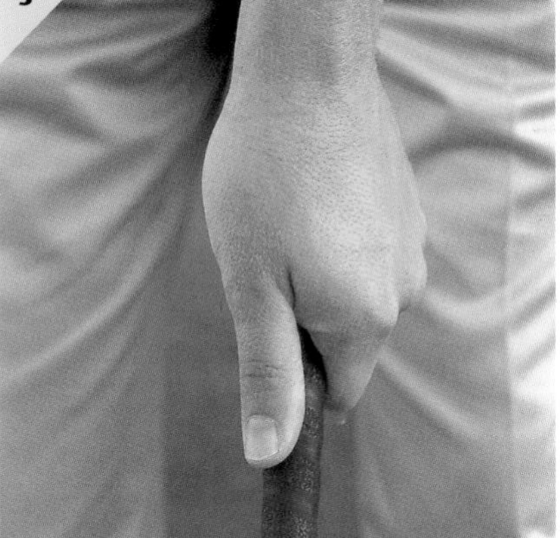

3 Now place your left thumb slightly to the right of the shaft so that your left wrist joint is now directly on top of the club handle. This is important because if it is done correctly, the joints of your shoulder, elbow and wrist line up with the club face to square it up at impact.

A good *grip*

From this unusual angle, you can see the fundamentals of a good grip as shown by Lanny Wadkins. The handle is cradled in the lower palm and fingers of the left hand, and the knuckles of both hands are in a line. Notice also the beautiful firmness without tension. He has a "hold" on the club rather than a strangulation grip.

How tight *is right?*

Checking your grip pressure to make sure that it is correct is an important part of a good swing. If you squeeze the club to death, you can't cock your wrists correctly and this denies you the power source created when your left arm and your club shaft form a 90-degree angle during the backswing. If you grip it too lightly, your brain will sense it and at some point in your swing, you will have to re-grip to maintain control.

Now it is true that the "effective" weight of your club changes as the speed of the club head increases. This requires an adjustment in grip pressure as your club head approaches the ball but that's all done automatically. Fortunately, all you have to do is to start with the correct pressure and your brain will take care of the rest.

Your goal is to hold the club exerting equal pressure with both hands. Your grip pressure should be firm enough to control the weight of the club, but not so tight that movement is inhibited. On a scale of one to ten where ten is very tight, your pressure on normal shots should be in the five range.

The grip *continued*

Your right-hand grip

- Your right hand comes in from the side with the palm facing in the direction you want the ball to go.
- The handle is held in the fingers of your right hand with the two pads of the right hand forming a pocket to accommodate the left thumb.
- When your right hand is closed on the club, your thumb and index finger should form a trigger. Your right thumb is to the left of the shaft.
- With this configuration your right palm should be facing both your left palm and the target. The thumb of your left hand fits in the pocket of your right palm.

Check points

Once both hands are on the club, you can check to see if your right hand is on the club correctly by simply extending your right index finger down the shaft. If your index finger extends exactly down the side of the shaft so that the shaft is between your index finger and the target, your right hand is in a good position. You will know that your right hand is incorrectly positioned if your index finger is either on top or underneath the shaft.

An excellent check point for a correct left hand grip is the positioning of your "anatomical snuff box," the small pocket at the base of your thumb between your wrist and hand. It should be directly over the center of the club handle because when centrifugal force pulls your arms straight through impact, your wrist joint (snuff box), elbow joint and shoulder joint will seek alignment. If you want a square club face at impact, those three joints need to be in alignment at address.

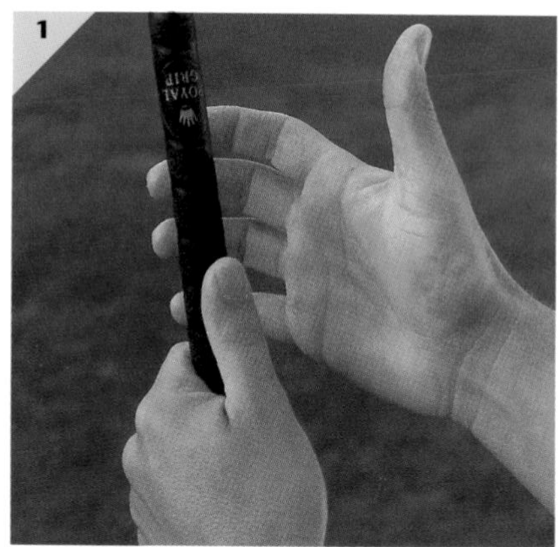

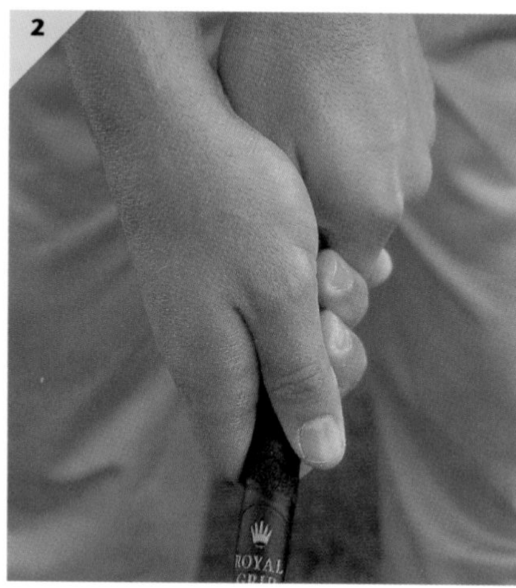

1 Let your right hand approach the club from the side rather than from above or below.

2 The "V's" formed by your thumbs and index fingers are parallel and point to your right cheek.

Ball position

The second fundamental is ball position. A correctly positioned ball is a prerequisite for square contact. The location of the golf ball affects both your shoulder alignment and the steepness of your swing. If the golf ball is too far forward in your stance (toward your target foot), your chest must turn toward the target so that you can sole your club head behind the ball. This "opens" your shoulders and because the club swings where the shoulders point, you're stuck with a slicer's swing path—steep and outside-to-in.

If you locate the ball too far back in your stance (toward your trail foot) then your chest must point to the right of the target, closing your shoulders and creating a flat, inside-to-out swing path. That's not what you want either.

1 With the ball too far forward, your shoulders align left of the target promoting a slice.

2 With the ball back in your stance, your shoulders align right of the target, the prelude to a hook.

3 Depending on the club, the ball moves about three ball widths from your left cheek, to your logo and finally to your armpit.

1

2

3

The bottom of your arc

With an iron, your club face contacts the ball just before it reaches the bottom of its arc. When the ball is teed with a wood, contact takes place at the bottom of the arc or slightly on the upswing. Since your left hand is higher on the club than your right hand and you are on your left leg at impact, the bottom of the arc is opposite your left armpit.

Thus for your driver, the ball will be positioned opposite your left armpit, guaranteeing that the club will travel level to the ground at impact. With your long irons and fairway woods, locate the ball off your logo and with the medium to short irons, the ball will be positioned farther back opposite your left cheek.

Ball position *continued*

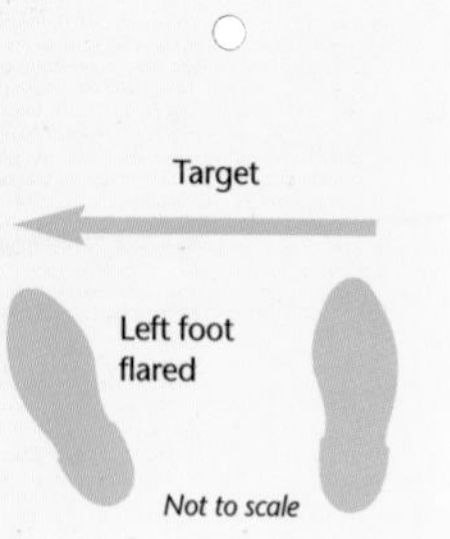

Don't use your feet

Target

Left foot flared

Not to scale

Flaring your feet can distort your perception of your ball position.

Always relate your ball position to your upper body: feet are a poor reference, since most golfers use their toes to judge ball position and they can give you the illusion that the ball position is correct when, in fact, it is not.

You can see how easy it is to be fooled by trying out the following: place a ball in the middle of your stance opposite the mid-line of your body. Now when you draw your right foot back about five inches the ball appears to have moved forward. When you open your stance the ball appears to "back up" just as it does when you flare your left foot out.

Checking ball position

Once you have set up to the ball, the way to check your ball position is to straighten your spine until the golf club has been lifted to waist high and is parallel to the ground.

- If your ball position is correct, your shoulders will be square and the club shaft will be perpendicular to the target line.
- With the ball too far forward, your shoulders will be open, and the shaft will be angled to the left of the ball.
- With the ball too far back, your shoulders will be closed, and the shaft will be angled to the right of the ball.

Aim and alignment

Aim and alignment are both defined in terms of the target line, an imaginary line connecting the target to the ball.

- **Aim** refers to the direction in which your club face points in relation to the target line. When it looks to the left, it is said to be "closed"; when it points to the right, it is "open"; and when it looks directly at the target, the club face is termed "square."
- **Alignment,** on the other hand, always refers to the direction your body faces. When it looks to the left of the target line, it is open; to the right, it is closed; and when the imaginary lines connecting your shoulders, hips and feet are parallel to the target line, then you have a square body alignment.

The key here is to begin all normal full shots from a square set up position with regard to both your club face and your body. Your shoulders determine the direction in which your arms swing, so they must be aligned correctly to ensure that your club face looks at the target at impact.

Because it is your club face that makes contact with the ball, where it is pointing at impact determines the direction in which the golf ball will travel. It is helpful to use the lines on the toe and heel formed by the grooves on your club face for aiming. It may sound simplistic but you must take

Weight *distribution*

When your ball is teed with your driver and three wood, your weight distribution favors your right side (about 60 percent), but with the rest of your clubs you start with a 50:50 distribution. From front to back, your weight should be spread evenly from the balls of your feet to your heels with the majority of weight focused on the inside edges of your feet.

Aiming your club face

An open club face aims right of target.

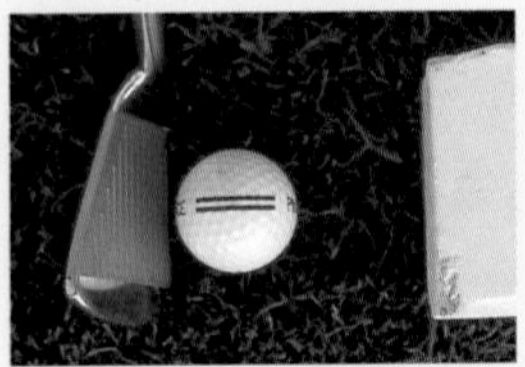

A square club face aims down the target line.

A closed club face aims left of target.

great care to aim your club face at the target.

The alignment of your hips is especially important because they dictate the amount of rotation away from and back to the ball. Open hips will restrict the backswing and cause you to open them too much through impact. However, closed hips will cause an over-rotation on the backswing and make it hard to get your hips turned back in time for impact.

In and of itself, your foot position is the least important of the body alignments, but because the position of the feet can influence the position of both your shoulders and hips, they should be in line parallel with the target line.

1 In a good set up, the body will be aligned parallel left of the target line and the club face is aimed square to the target line.

2 Use the aiming lines on your club to properly square your club face to your target.

What does *"Square" mean?*

The term "square" is rarely explained. To understand this key concept lay down four clubs as follows:

- One club along the target line.
- One club along your foot line parallel to the target line.
- One club from your left heel perpendicular to the target line.
- One club from your right heel also perpendicular to the target line.

The four clubs form a square. Your feet, knees, hips and your shoulders are square, as is your club face. Creating the square shows the relationships of the geometry between your body, the club face, the ball and the target line.

Flexibility

The amount of hip and shoulder rotation during your backswing depends on how flexible you are. The less flexible you are, the more flared your right foot should be to allow you more turn. The more flexible you are, the less your right foot should be flared to prevent you from over-turning.

Stance width

Finding the correct stance width provides you with a stable platform on which to swing. How you set your feet at address depends on your body build and which club you're hitting.

Foot width

The width of your stance influences your stability, balance and mobility. The widest your foot spread should be is shoulder width apart; the narrowest is the width of your hips. A good way to check your stance width for a mid iron is to turn into your follow through position and if your knees reach each other your stance is the correct width.

- If your knees cannot reach each other, your stance is too wide.
- If they overlap, your stance is too narrow.

Foot flare

When your left foot is flared out at address, it is easier to rotate your left hip and knee correctly as you swing through the hitting zone. To find your ideal amount of flare, experiment with hitting some balls with the left foot flared out at different angles.

- Start with your left foot turned out about 25 degrees (a quarter of a turn) and allow the quality of your golf shots to determine how much flare you need.
- If your left foot is flared out too much, your shot pattern will be weak fades.
- If the left foot is too square, the shot pattern will be low pull hooks.

1 If your right knee passes your left, your stance is too narrow.

2 Your stance width is correct when your knees are even with one another.

3 If your right knee can't meet your left knee your stance is too wide.

Posture

Posture affects not only your balance but also your swing plane. When your posture is too upright, you'll swing the club in an exaggerated curve around you that results in a hook or a pulled shot. When you're bent over too much, you'll pick the club up producing an abbreviated backswing that's so abrupt that it virtually guarantees sliced shots.

Knee flex

Your knees are designed to bend your body backward. Your knee flex should match the knee bend of your normal walking stride just as your forward foot flattens on the ground. This is your natural balance flex point and it differs from golfer to golfer, depending on flexibility and body physique.

The amount of knee flex is also related to the length of your arms. With proper posture, golfers with short arms require more knee flex than those with longer arms.

No matter how much knee flex you have, make sure that your weight is evenly spread from the balls of your feet to your heels and never on your toes.

Bending from the hips

Your body is designed to bend forward from the hips, not the waist. When you bend from your waist, you hunch your back and de-activate your centers of rotation. Your hip joints lock up, thus forcing your hips to move laterally, producing a slide instead of a turn.

By bending from your hips, your arms will hang, tension-free, directly below your shoulders. This also creates room for your arms to swing, and it will establish your swing plane.

Notice that when you assume the correct position, your abdomen is retracted upward and inward causing your backside to protrude. Remember that with your spine angled correctly, the weight of your head and shoulders pulls you forward toward the ball during your golf swing and it is your protruding backside that provides the counterweight to keep you in balance.

To get the feeling of the position, imagine that you are about to sit on an above-the-waist, three-legged stool. The traditional image of a regular-height stool causes too much knee bend with a squatting appearance.

Shoulders

The shoulder level check point features your arms hanging straight down from your shoulders with your upper arms adhering lightly to your body as if they were strapped on top of your chest. You're in the correct position when you can drop the club at address, relax your arms and they don't change their angle of hang.

Head
posture

Your head should be positioned in the middle of your shoulders with your chin held high in the proud position. If you let it rest on your chest, it blocks your shoulder turn. The proud position requires you to "peep" at the ball with the bottom of your eyes rather than stare at it with a droopy head.

Posture *continued*

Posture drill

1 With straight knees, place a shaft across your hips, parallel to the ground.

2 Now push the shaft backwards until your backside protrudes and your weight moves to your toes.

3 Then flex your knees until your weight is redistributed from the balls of your feet back to your heels.

Summary

Once you're in the correct posture, the top of your spine, the tip of your elbows, your knees and the balls of the feet will be in a straight line. You will be in that universal athletic position similar to a quarterback taking a snap, a tennis player waiting to return a serve or a swimmer ready to make a racing dive. The overall set up position is one of springy readiness so that if there was a pit of snakes between you and your ball, you could leap over it without rearranging your body before you spring.

Useful tip

If you can avoid it, don't wear bifocals when you play golf because they will force you to drop your head in order to see the ball.

Pre-shot routine

The pre-shot routine is often perceived as something you do just before you swing but which does not have much relation to the golf swing. But it is part and parcel of the swing and, however personalized it might be, no expert player is without one.

The advantages of a good pre-shot routine are numerous. A good routine calms you down because you're doing the same things in the same order for every shot. This protects you against the tendency to disrupt your rhythm under stress by either speeding up or taking too much time.

When you develop a solid routine, you'll be insulated from outside distractions like noise and people moving around while you're trying to hit your ball. And as we shall see in the next chapter, once under way, your pre-shot routine is like an avalanche culminating in that special feeling called a "go" signal which allows you to pull the trigger with confidence.

The routine

Good golf shots are a combination of correct distance and direction, but you'll confuse your brain if you make it think about both while you swing. This is why you need a pre-shot routine that will separate the two, for each and every shot.

Take care of direction by aiming your club face and aligning your body correctly at address. Once this is done, forget about the direction of your golf shot and let your golf swing produce the correct distance your shot needs to travel. Design your routine so that you fix the direction first, then the distance—and always in that sequence.

1 Stand behind your ball and plan your shot. Make sure that your practice swing is a true rehearsal of the up-coming shot by taking it in the direction of the target, off a similar lie, and at the same speed as the swing you are about to make. Once you've pictured the shot in your mind and made a practice swing, take a deep breath to relax.

2 Now step into your address position with your right foot leading the way. Before you bring your left foot into position, sole your club face behind the ball, so that it points at the target. Then, keeping your club head in the same position, bring your left foot into position so that your body is perpendicular to your club face. You have now locked in your direction.

3 From this position, take one look at the target to finalize your distance calculation by rotating your head without lifting it, waggle and pull the trigger, allowing the speed of your swing to produce the correct distance.

Note:

This procedure will take only about 30 to 45 seconds and if you make it a habit, then your priorities will be correct for every shot: direction through address, distance through swing speed.

Chapter three

Your golf swing

In this chapter, we describe the entire swing in detail based on our belief that your golf swing will be no better than your concept of what a good swing should be. If you know what to do and this is clear and distinct in your mind, you'll be able to do it.

Whether you're a beginner, setting about building your swing from scratch, or an experienced player who needs to rebuild your swing, don't confuse comfort with correct. When you're learning something new, it usually doesn't feel right at first, and since you're accustomed to doing it incorrectly, your brain will label the correct way as wrong. We call this uncomfortable transition time an "incubation period" and in learning any motor skill it depends on how perfectly you do it and how many times you repeat it before your new skill becomes a habit.

US Open Champion Ernie Els finishes another flawless swing. The balanced, dynamic finish is indicative of all that went before.

Don't let the ball be your master

Another sound piece of advice when you're learning to make a golf swing is: don't let the ball be your master. When it is your master, you make changes in your swing based solely on how much you liked the previous shot. But when ball flight (high, low, slice, hook etc.) is your only evaluation system for how well you're learning, you'll spend most of your time tinkering with your swing to get the ball to go straight rather than learning each piece of your swing sequentially.

Remember, when you're learning a swing piece, such as the grip, your evaluation system for success is how well you're matching the model grip, not where the ball goes. You might have six more changes to make in your swing before you can expect the ball to go where you want.

Play golf, not "golf swing"

The swing mechanics presented in this section give you the information you need to build your swing, but this information is not for thinking about while you're actually playing the game.

On the practice tee, you break your swing down and work on its parts but when it's all said and done, you need to put Humpty Dumpty back together again, forget about your swing and go *play* golf. You are now ready to develop the blueprint for your swing and we begin with several key concepts that apply to all swings, no matter how personalized.

The plane angle

The plane angle of your golf swing is the tilt or angle that your club shaft creates with the ground both at address and also as you swing the club.

Each club in your bag has a different shaft angle so if you carry 14 clubs you have 14 different swing plane angles. Your five iron, assuming it's correctly soled, creates an angle with the ground of 62 degrees, whereas your nine iron has a shaft angle of 66 degrees. This means that your swing with your nine iron will be more upright than with your five, and your five iron much more upright than your driver (55 degrees).

Thus the plane angle of each swing is established by the club you choose for the shot, and each time you change clubs, you change the angle of your swing. Don't worry about this; you don't have to consciously adjust your swing because the correct progression of shaft angles is built into your clubs at the factory. Just take your address correctly as described in the previous section and you'll at least start with a perfect plane angle—it's called being "on plane."

The trick, of course, is to stay on plane from start to finish. In essence, everything you do in terms of weight shift, shoulder rotation, wrist set and all the other in-swing mechanics is dedicated to keeping your club shaft on plane; if you can do this, you're well on your way to playing better golf.

Axis

Your golf swing is a three-axis affair composed of your spine, around which your upper body moves, and your left and right hip joints, around which, each in their turn, your entire body rotates.

While you are swinging, your goal is be "in" the correct hip socket at the correct time. Being "in" means you have established that hip joint as the center of rotation by shifting weight into it and then turning your body around it. Remember that your hip must be over its corresponding heel in order for it to rotate. Thus every good swing has a hip switch.

When your club head is moving away from the ball, weight flows into your right hip joint. When your club head is moving toward the target, pressure flows into your left hip joint.

Leverage

Levers are multipliers of power. Your body and your club form your lever system, and when you use your hands and arms correctly, angles of power are created through which the energy produced by coil is increased before being released at impact.

For example, during your swing away from the ball an important power angle is created when your wrists cock forming a 90-degree angle between your left arm and the club shaft.

Another important power angle comes from the same angle that you create at the elbow to throw a ball. This is called the "Power V" and it is one of the most powerful levers in the human body. When it snaps open—in other words, when your right arm suddenly straightens during the downswing—it serves as the key multiplier of the energy generated by the large muscles of your legs and trunk.

Swing path

At the start of your backswing, the club head travels directly back from the ball on the extended line of the target and continues in a gently flowing arc both inward and upward. If you picture a large tilted wheel, with your neck as the hub, and the ball at the point where the wheel touches the ground, you will get an idea of the backswing path.

The path your club head takes as you swing back to the ball is underneath the backswing path so that your club head approaches the ball from inside the target line. The backswing starts the club head down the target line, and the downswing returns it inside the target line. The rotation of your body then squares the club at impact. As your body continues its turn through impact the club head will again move inside the target line. So the proper path is: **inside—square—inside.**

The most common violation of this **inside to square to inside** path occurs when you start your downswing with your right shoulder moving out toward the target line, creating an outside-to-in slicer's path.

On your downswing, let your club head follow the path of the balls to create an inside to square path.

Coil is *a ratio*

To coil correctly you must set one part of your body against the other so that torque is produced. When you turn your shoulders more than your hips during your backswing you stretch the big, banded muscles of your back, pelvis and thighs and this tautness turns into club head speed on the way back to the ball as you uncoil through impact.

Unfortunately, too many golfers are so intent on turning that they never coil. If you turn your hips and shoulders the same amount you never produce any resistance which is why we say that there's a turn in every coil but not a coil in every turn. If you turn your shoulders 90 degrees, you turn your hips about 45 degrees; if you only turn your shoulders 80 degrees, you should try for a 40-degree hip turn.

Sequence

Even if you coil correctly, there are often times when you release your coil too early, causing power to leak out before it can be used at impact. Thus there is an optimum sequence to your swing, one that first generates, then transmits and finally delivers the power to your golf ball right on time. This sequence of moves and swing positions is called proper sequential motion (PSM) and it represents the concept that when you do something is as important as what you do.

Impact

While you know the ecstasy of success and the emotional pain of failure, your ball knows only impact. There are five characteristics of impact that control your ball flight:

- What the face of your club is doing through impact.
- The path of your club.
- The angle of approach of your club head.
- The speed of the club head.

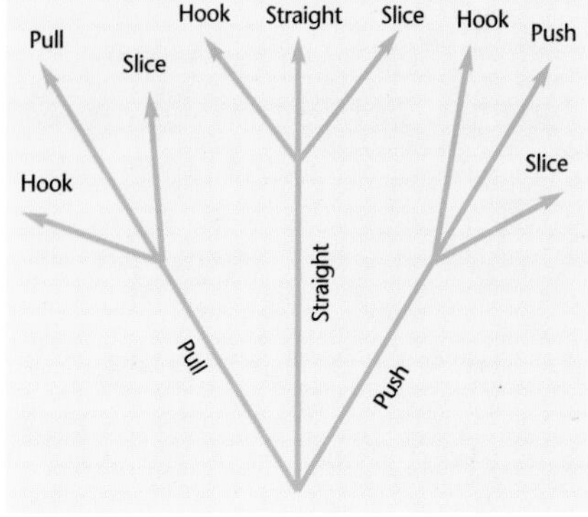

- Where on the club face you hit the ball.

With regard to direction, there are nine ball flights possible, as illustrated above.

In general the path on which your club face is moving at impact influences the direction in which your ball starts; it may start left of target (a pull), to the right of your target (a push) or go straight at the target.

What your club face is doing through impact influences both the starting direction and the spin of the ball.

- If your club face is held open in relation to its path, your ball will curve from left to right.
- If the club face is in the process of closing, your ball will curve from right to left.
- If your club face is square to its path, your ball will fly with minimal curve.

Tempo

This is a key to striking consistently good golf shots and it's your hips that control your tempo. In the golf swing, the rotary speed of your hips governs how fast your arms and club head move. By turning your hips at a constant rate, your club head speed increases incrementally during your swing. Remember that as you coil you're creating multipliers of speed called levers, and these are "operated" by your hips.

To better understand how the tempo of your hip turn controls your swing, imagine a skate line at an ice show. The skaters are holding hands as the middle skater (the hub skater) begins to spin. Each skater picks up the motion from the preceding skater and adds to it, so the farther from the center a skater is, the faster she's moving and the more distance she travels as the line revolves. The hub skater controls the entire line and as she increases her spin rate, the skater at the end of the line moves faster and faster.

The hub skater represents your hips, and as you progress out from the hub, each skater represents a club in your bag. The longer the shaft of the club, the farther the club head is from the hub of your swing and thus the faster it moves. By allowing your hips to move at the same speed in both directions with every club in the bag, you can develop a swing tempo that is the same for every club. Your "hub tempo" stays constant and you produce the different distances you need to play the game by simply changing clubs. With this in mind you can see how the effortless power of the expert player is tied to good tempo.

To find your natural tempo, note the speed of your walk. If your gait is quick, your hip turn should also be rapid. If your stride is slow and deliberate, your hip turn should match it.

Club face *and path*

Club face and path, combined with the other three characteristics, dictate your ball flight, and if you know how they affect your shot pattern, you can troubleshoot your swing.

For example, if your ball slices, then the club face was open at impact relative to the path of the club. If you push the ball straight to the right of target, your swing path was too much from in-to-out with the face of your club square to the path. If you top the ball, then your swing was too vertical ("V"-shaped), causing your club head to catch the top of the ball. And if you pop up your tee shot, then you probably swung the club down on too steep an angle from out-to-in.

The swing in sequence

For analysis, your swing away from the ball is divided into two phases:

- The backswing where your club starts back from the ball creating width and leverage.
- The upswing where your club elevates to the top of your swing generating the height and arc you need for power.

Your return to the ball is composed of:

- The downswing as your club moves downward from the top of your swing, retaining the angles of power developed in the backswing.
- The forward swing during which you deliver your power at impact by releasing your club head to the ball.

Each phase is distinctly different, and an understanding of how the phases differ and what goes on in each will help you in assembling the blueprint of your golf swing.

The backswing

In the short span from address to the end of your backswing the width of your swing is established. For our purposes, width is the distance your club head moves away from the ball down your toe line.

Width is important to your swing because a good golf swing requires a certain amount of space where you can move your arms and club. Without this space, you'll be too cramped with no room for the club to travel on its proper path.

Starting your swing

1 In the section on the set up we saw that your left arm was on top of and tight to your chest. Now to start your swing your left arm simply slides across your chest until it reaches

1

2

its full length and can move no further on its own without pulling your left shoulder with it. At this point you "run out of left arm" and it is the momentum of your arm swing that starts your shoulder turn by pulling your left shoulder down and away from the target.

2 At the same time that your left arm starts its move across your chest, your weight transfers into your right hip joint preparing it for rotation. Your right elbow bends slightly and moves several inches down the toe line from its original position at address. Here the shaft of your club is directly above your toe line with the face of the club matching the tilt of your spine. This position signals the end of your backswing.

The upswing

1 Once your backswing is complete, all that remains to be done is to turn your chest away from the target allowing your left shoulder to move under your chin and your right shoulder to move behind your neck. The folding action of your elbow is similar to the motion you make when you throw a ball. At this point, the weight of the club head swinging upward from the ball causes your right wrist to hinge back toward your right forearm while your left wrist remains flat. This is known as "cocking" the wrists and at this point all the important relationships have been established for your on-plane swing to the top.

2 Note that your right hip should turn over your right heel but no further. To prevent overturning your hips, keep your right knee flexed just as it was at address.

The one-piece *upswing*

Note: During the upswing, everything moves as a unit (club shaft, arms, shoulders, chest and hips) to ensure proper coiling and prevent any independent lifting of your arms and hands.

This one-piece upswing and its companion, the one-piece forward swing, is what gives today's rotational golf swing its quiet, simple look. In the modern swing there are no unsightly angles to catch your eye and, since they move as a unit, no specific body part stands out.

A note on *shoulder tilt*

At address your shoulders are parallel to the target line with your left shoulder higher than your right by the same amount that your left hand is above your right on the golf club. In-swing your shoulders rotate in a circle around your neck. As you swing away from the ball, your left shoulder moves down and under your chin while your right shoulder rotates behind and over your neck. At the top of your swing and just after impact, a line connecting your shoulders would be tilted at the same angle as your club shaft. Thus your shoulders tilt as they rotate because your spine is tilted at address. Coming back to the ball, your shoulders reverse the circle as the left retraces its path back through its starting point at address to a position over and behind your neck while your right shoulder travels downward and under your neck.

The top of the swing

1 At the top of the swing you're fully coiled with your club shaft perpendicular to the line of your shoulders and your shoulder incline matching the plane angle of your club shaft at address. Your club is supported by the palm of your right hand as if you were carrying a tray. Your elbows are level so that an imaginary line connecting them is parallel to the ground.

2 Your right leg is flexed with 80 percent of your weight supported by your right hip joint and leg. The distribution of weight in your right foot should be from the balls of your feet to the heel, favoring the inside rim of your right foot. Avoid feeling that your weight is on your toes or leaking over the outside of your right foot.

1

2

Your return swing

Just as your swing away from the ball had two distinct phases, so does your return swing. The first phase is the downswing in which your left arm drops back down your chest as your right elbow begins to straighten. Once your club is in position, your forward swing begins, allowing your turn to square the club head to the ball at impact.

Your downswing

As in everything else you do on this planet, gravity plays an important part in your golf swing. Your upswing must overcome the force of gravity but once your club reaches the top of your swing, it's poised to take advantage of the very force (gravity) that was working against it just a moment before—if you let it.

The move that starts your downswing is really two moves: one lower body and one upper body. At the same time that your left arm slides back down your chest retracing the exact route it took during your upswing, your weight transfers into your left hip joint beginning your lower body turn back to the ball. This establishes your left hip as the center of rotation, allowing your swing arc to flatten out just before impact so that you can make solid contact.

You have probably noticed by now that your downswing is just the reverse of your backswing. In both, your left arm moves across your chest as your weight flows into the correct hip: right on the backswing and left on the downswing. A good swing is therefore symmetrical both back and through.

The angle *of power*

Note: There are two important points that you should remember concerning your downswing.

- The first is that while your left arm slides down your chest and your right arm straightens, you maintain the 90-degree angle between your left forearm and the club shaft. This is an angle of power that must be held until the impact zone.
- The second is that during your downswing, your back is still to the target, a prerequisite for preventing "over-the-top." The premature movement of your chest pulls your club head on to the target line much too early.

One-piece
takeaway

The "one-piece takeaway" used by some golfers demands that you start everything (club, hands, arms, shoulders, chest and hips) together away from the ball, but if you're not careful, you'll turn your hands and club inside your toe line too quickly, ruining your coil and fouling your swing plane. This is why we recommend a sequence of moves starting with your left arm during your takeaway and then a one-piece "upswing" where your club is elevated to the top of your swing by simply turning your chest against your resisting lower body. It is much safer and produces more coil when you get your swing under way with your left arm moving across your chest as your weight shifts into your right hip.

The forward swing to impact

Once your left arm has dropped the club into position and you have established your left hip joint as your pivot center, you're ready to release your right side. At this point in the swing you have about 80 percent of your weight on your left side ready to act as a buttress or wall of resistance against which you will hit.

The key here is that while your left side, from the knee down, stops to form the wall that you hit against at impact, your entire right side must continue its motion so that it can smack full force into that wall. This collision gives you a powerful, well-timed release. The concept that cues the right side of your body during your forward swing is that everything that is moving should keep on moving.

1 Just before impact your left hip has rotated behind you, increasing the pulling force on your club head. Your left arm is straight with your bent right arm under it, a position that holds your wrist cock till the very last instant.

2 Now, in a split second, your right arm fully straightens, emptying the pent-up power down the shaft and into the ball.

Follow through to finish

If you've kept your chest and right side moving as they should through the hitting zone, just after impact the force of rotation will pull both arms straight so that the club head will line up in the middle of your chest.

After impact, let your body rotate upward around your spine without any feeling of restriction in your left or right side. Allow the force of the right shoulder turning through impact to gradually rotate your head toward the target so that you are looking "under" the ball as it speeds away. In other words, allow your body to fully release through the ball, neither adding anything nor holding anything back.

1 Both arms reach full extension through impact.

2 After impact, the shaft and club head are in front of the chest.

3 The right side releases fully through the ball producing a perfectly balanced follow through.

There are four criteria for a well balanced finish:

- Your full body weight is on your left side.
- You are standing at your full height.
- The front of your body including your right knee is pointing at the target.
- You are on your right toe, using your back foot as a rudder.

"U" Vs. "V"

Super slow-motion film shows that the club face skims the ground as the swing arc flattens through impact so that the energy in the club face is delivered through the ball toward the target rather than down into the ground or up into the sky. Your best swings are therefore "U"-shaped with a flattening at the bottom of the swing rather than in the shape of a "V".

But when you fail to shift your weight to your left side to start the downswing, you're trapped on your right side and then your swing becomes "V"-shaped. This is why you must start the downswing by repositioning your weight onto your left side.

Chapter four

Star swings

In an effort to gain consistency, and a lower ball flight with less backspin, Greg Norman has changed from a classic to a more modern swing.

Understanding how star swings develop can help you to build your own swing. The golf swing is made up of swing elements, such as grip, posture, ball position, takeaway etc., and the question is how do you put these elements together to play your best golf? Which stars do you pick as your models and what swing elements do you appropriate from them for your own purposes?

It's obvious that the swings of, say, Colin Montgomerie and Steve Elkington do not look the same, yet they are both star players. And while categorization always does a disservice to someone, it is possible to explain how the two swings could look so dissimilar yet get such good results. To do this we can divide the star swings into two categories: the classic and the modern.

As you will gather from the accompanying chart, those golfers with a classic swing take the club away in one piece and swing it on an upright plane high above them with a long flowing arc. They exhibit a lot of lateral hip motion and their follow through is characterized by the bent spine of the Reverse C position, giving the impression that they sling the club head out from under them.

Those with a modern swing start the club away with their left arm and swing the club on a flatter plane more around them in a tight, rounded arc. Their hip turn is predominantly rotational and they enter the follow through section of their swing more erect, having unwound their coil around their spine. They whirl the club head around them.

However, as we are about to see, just when you think these distinctions are hard and fast you find a glaring divergence, such as Montgomerie, a classic swinger, adopting the ball position of the modern swing. The existence of this cross-pollination of swing elements from one swing type to the other prompts two basic observations: the first is that good golf swings, in order to satisfy the laws of physics (which they all must do), evolve based on body type, personality, the demands of the environment, and often, although not always, under the watchful eye of a masterful teacher. Thus swing elements are assembled based on the individual differences of the player.

The second observation is that the definition of error in a golf swing is not always an objective fact carved on a stone tablet that applies to every swing mechanic and every golf swing. We believe you'll agree after analyzing our star swings that before you label a movement or a position as incorrect, and therefore set about to change it, you must show that it does not fit in with the rest of the movements and positions that make up the golf swing. The odds are that if you put a bag over his head so no one would recognize him and had him hit into a net so they couldn't see the ball flight, 95 percent of the teaching professionals would change Lee Trevino's looping, push-fade swing, thereby preserving his early career as a bag room attendant at Horizon Golf Club in El Paso, Texas.

It's fashionable to use the phrase "compensating errors" to describe any deviation from the so-called perfect, and it is usually spoken in the sad tone reserved for someone who has a debilitating disease as in "poor thing, he has compensating errors." But what would we give for the "compensating errors" of a Ben Crenshaw, a Johnny Miller or a Colin Montgomerie? As an example, Montgomerie's back ball position is not an error because it fits his golf game, producing the ball flight he needs: low and left to right. Remember that he plays worldwide in some fierce wind and if he moved his ball forward he'd hit the ball higher, exposing his fade to a wind that would turn it into a slice.

	Classic swing	**Modern swing**
Ball position	Forward	Back
Grip	Weak to neutral	Strong to neutral
Hips back	Tilted/back leg straight	Level
Hip motion	Lateral then rotational	Purely rotational
Takeaway	One-piece simultaneous: chest, hands and club head	Sequential: arm swing then wrist set, then shoulder turn
Backswing	High arcing/up and over	Flatter/rounded
Right foot position	Perpendicular to the target line	Flared
Hand/forearm action	Integral	Minimal
Legs	Active	Quiet
Release	Slinging action	Rotational body release
Finish	Reverse C	Straight spine

Note:
1 The elements cross pollinate.
2 In categorizing a particular player you'll find they have many features of one swing style but very few have all. The variations occur depending on the conditions of play, body build, temperament, natural tendencies and external influences. Golf swings are built by finding basic elements that fit together.

Your golf *blueprint*

In the chapter on the golf swing we gave you an excellent blueprint from which to begin to build your swing but when you have finished adapting it to your own needs, it may not look anything like your original blueprint. The important concept here is that your overall golf game is greater than your golf swing so you may introduce something in your swing, such as a weak grip, based not on whether it is objectively correct, classic or modern but on how it links up with your other strengths and weaknesses and, ultimately, how it improves your ability to score.

The Miller *grip*

The Miller grip has always played a big role in his success and he has coined the phrase "impact fix" to describe his wrist position: the back of his left hand and his forearm are fixed in a straight line and stay that way from start to finish. When you lose this straight line relationship, the left wrist collapses, altering the effective loft of the golf club and thereby affecting not only the direction but how far the ball goes.

In his glory years, Miller kept the relationship between the back of his left hand, forearm and the club face constant all the way through his swing, which enabled him to hit accurate irons that were often pin high. Although no statistics were kept, he, along with Byron Nelson, was probably pin high more often than any other player.

Johnny Miller The classic swing

Twenty years after his first victory at Pebble Beach, Johnny Miller stunned the golf world with a victory at the 1994 AT&T National Pro-Am at Pebble Beach. Injury to his knees prematurely ended his full-time playing career but, in his prime, Johnny Miller was unarguably the best player in the world. He won his first major, the 1973 US Open at Oakmont, in a decisive five-stroke victory with a final round 63, still the lowest score in major championship history. In 1974 and 1975, he set a blistering pace, winning 12 tournaments, posting 23 top ten finishes and two international victories. At Royal Birkdale in 1976, Johnny Miller defeated Jack Nicklaus and Seve Ballesteros by six strokes to claim the Open Championship. He was also at home in the desert where he won 13 titles, four at Tucson, and in 1975 when he won at Phoenix by 14 strokes.

1 The first impression is one of a beautifully balanced set up position; nothing is out of place here. The right shoulder is under the left by the same amount that his right hand is below his left on the club handle. In his youth his right foot was perpendicular to the line but now, to accommodate decreased flexibility, it's modestly flared. With the driver, his weight is distributed about 60 percent on the right and 40 percent on the left.

The forward ball position is an important element that controls his hip action once his swing begins. There's a dramatic flare of his left foot to encourage him to turn aggressively through the ball. With this amount of flare he must position the ball well forward in his stance to accommodate the dramatic leg drive that's characteristic of his swing.

2 Known for his early set of the angle, Miller actually sets it quickly but he does not set it early in his takeaway as indicated by the frame where his hands are on his right leg and the club head is still well below his hands. At this point his weight is already well into his right hip.

The biggest difference in Miller's swing today is that his hips and shoulders turn more level and his swing is much shorter than in his heyday. Now he suffers some bouts of wildness and off-center hitting because his level turn hip doesn't quite match the rest of his upright swing. Unless compensations are made, level hips match well with a shallow swing, while tilted hips match up with a steep swing.

3 Miller is an "up and down" swinger rather than a rotational swinger. By the time his left arm is parallel to the ground, the club head has been set well above the hands. There is not much hip turn and, as he coils into his right hip joint, his club head has moved upward rather than behind him, a relatively steep track that's perfect for iron play.

4 **5** Starting down, Miller tucks his right elbow in close to his side and has a terrific amount of right knee drive, keeping his right foot planted late into the downswing. Notice the beautiful knee flex that changes just before impact as the left leg straightens. It is this that gives him the characteristic "up and out" look which is so defining of his swing even now. The upward spiral of his body is responding to the posting of his left leg and because he has bad knees he relieves the pressure by spinning his left foot out to the left of the target.

6 The finish is also a trademark: a Reverse C with high hands that end up between his left shoulder and ear, indicating that the club stayed on the target line long after impact.

Miller has always maintained that playing from a Reverse C position allows him to keep the club head going through to the target longer. With the forward ball position, a major swing characteristic is a great deal of lateral movement which also helps keeps the club face on line longer and, if done correctly, leads to the Reverse C or comma position.

1
2
3
4
5
6

John Daly The classic swing

John Daly rocketed to stardom after his surprise victory at the 1991 PGA Championship at Crooked Stick and since then has recorded many wins on Tour. His super-long swing, explosive distance and mercurial personality fascinate his huge, rambunctious galleries, the size of which are reminiscent of Arnold Palmer's "Army". Lost in the shadows of Daly's phenomenal distance is his masterful touch around the greens, which he used to win his second major championship, the 1995 British Open at St Andrews. Daly remains a compelling figure wherever he plays, drawing massive galleries, even though he has not added to his two majors. In 1999, he teamed up with Laura Davies to win the JCPenney Classic after a play-off with Se Ri Pak and Paul Azinger.

1 At address he reaches for the ball to accommodate his large chest. He starts the swing with a one-piece move that keeps the club head lower longer than any of the modern tour players. As his left arm swings over his toe line, his hands begin to set the club very aggressively as his turn carries his club head well inside the toe line.

2 Notice that the writing on his glove is now facing the sky, indicating that as his wrists cock he's also rotating his left hand and forearm so that his club face looks upward. If his club face stayed this way, it would be dead shut at the top and he'd be a terrible hooker of the ball. But as he gets to the top of his swing the club face is pushed into a perfect position in relation to his shoulder plane by the elevation of his right elbow.

3 The angle of Daly's left arm at the top of his swing is an amazing feat of flexibility, impossible for the average person. Notice also that the trigger finger he uses helps to elongate his swing, as does his large amount of wrist cock.

4 With the club head traveling such an incredible distance the question is: what does Daly's body do in the meantime? Starting down he must find a way to slow his body to give his club time to get back in front of his body at impact. To give his club head a head start, Daly suspends himself on his right side like a ballerina, a clever solution to the time problem. The photos show that he begins his club head's return to the ball with his arms and shoulders before he shifts his weight to his left side. In this frame he's arrived at a position that looks like a normal tour player about to begin his downswing—and yet that club head has already traveled more than a foot back toward the ball.

5 The "flying right elbow" not only gives additional arc to his swing but it also serves a very important purpose in squaring the club face to his shoulder plane. During his downswing much of his power is gained by ratcheting up the speed of the club as he slams his right elbow back tight to his body, adding extra whip to the club through the impact zone.

To pull off his big swing he not only needs time: he also needs space. Note at the top of his swing how his head is located over his right foot, but as he starts down he pivots his head back toward the ball clearing space for his right shoulder so he can bring his right arm back to his right side.

6 During his swing he uses his legs as posts to coil around—the right leg on the backswing, the left on the forward swing. Through impact he hits across his left leg as the club swings by him.

Power *and timing*

Daly has the longest club head travel time in modern golf. He can swing back as far as he does because:

1 He's very flexible in his shoulder, hip and wrist joints.

2 He's a strong man whose body is used to swinging hard.

3 Each part of his technique (flying right elbow, high left arm, triggered index finger etc.) is perfectly suited to creating a huge arc.

Powerful as it is, his swing takes a great deal of timing to work correctly. He'll play superbly one or two weeks a year when his timing is perfect, overpowering the course and beating the entire field. When his timing is mediocre he'll be competitive and finish in the middle of the pack with the help of his beautiful short game and putting stroke. And when his timing is sub-par, he won't break 80.

1
2
3
4
5
6

Getting better *with age*

As Crenshaw has gotten older and his body less flexible, his accuracy off the tee has actually increased as he can no longer make those extra-long swings. Golf is probably the only game where, in some cases, you can get better as you age because as your body tightens up so does your swing. What Johnny Miller said about John Daly applies to all golfers with long swings: "When Daly is 90 his swing should be about normal."

Ben Crenshaw The classic swing

Ben Crenshaw captured his second Masters Tournament in 1995 in an emotion-filled week that began after serving as pall bearer at the funeral of his life-long teacher Harvey Pennick. As well as being a player with over 40 titles to his merit, and known as one of the best putters who ever played the game, Ben is also a respected golf course architect, noted golf historian and recipient of the distinguished Bob Jones Award in 1991. Despite setbacks from illness during his thirties, Crenshaw has produced a string of wins since turning forty and led the United States team to the Ryder Cup in 1999 with the greatest comeback in the event's history.

1 At the start, his feet are wide apart, a position that brings stability to the high, free-flowing swing that is about to occur. Crenshaw has a good deal of upper body movement in his swing, another reason for his wide stance—otherwise he'd lose his balance.

He puts a classic hold on the club with both palms facing one another, ensuring that they work together rather than fighting each other for control. The "Vs" formed by his index fingers and thumbs are parallel to one another, pointing to his right cheek. A fine grip like this one is one of the great gifts an instructor can bestow on a student, the effects of which last long after most in-swing advice has disappeared.

His right foot is perpendicular to the target line to ensure that the club swings up and over him rather than around behind him. The ball position is a bit back for a high ball hitter like Ben, and when his timing gets off, this may lead to the bouts of wildness that occasionally plague him.

He begins with a one-piece takeaway using his chest to move the unit composed of his arms, hands, shoulders and club. His right elbow stays straight for a long time, giving maximum extension of the club head away from his body. He is not a large man but he does hit the ball a good way due to his extension and the high arc of his swing.

2 At the top, he's well coiled with a high left arm whose tilt or angle matches that of his club shaft soled at address. Via tilted hips and a straightened (not stiff) right leg his club head is propelled high above him. You can see that a good deal of his weight is loaded in his right hip, and that his left foot is slightly off the ground, pulled up and back by the force of his coil.

3 He starts down to the ball with a lateral motion of his hips towards the target. This slots the club shaft behind him so he can come to the ball on an inside path. It's a much larger hip shuttle than in most players and gives the appearance that he is sliding, but this is only because his head and left shoulder have turned so far behind the ball (almost over his right foot) during the backswing. He is not sliding past the ball because his swing center, located just below his neck, stays behind the ball until well into his follow through.

4 Note that even with all the lateral hip motion, his spine stays fixed. If you draw a line from his hat to the tip of the tree in the background you can see that he turns around his neck once the downswing is under way.

5 In the impact frame of our swing sequence you can see Ben's left leg pants cuff flying forward as his lower leg plants in preparation for the release. Once again, he is a classic slinger of the club as he slams on the brakes with his left side to release the club.

6 In his finish position you see no wrinkles in his right shoe, indicating that he has fully released all his weight to the left. He appears to squeeze every ounce of power out of his swing using length of arc, rhythmically timed, as his major power source.

1
2
3
4
5
6

Hip
motion

In Montgomerie's formative years, the major shaper of his swing action was his hip motion. Sliders are usually faders of the ball, while rotators are usually drawers of the ball and, as a rule, it's very hard to change your hip action. So in most cases a golf swing evolves around the natural movement of the hips. It's likely that to keep the fade out of the wind, he moved the ball back in his stance and, with the ball back, he had to be careful not to hook it, so he cupped his wrist at the top of his swing to open the face.

Colin Montgomerie The classic swing

Colin Montgomerie has won the European Order of Merit for seven straight years, 1993 to 1999. He's the first man to do so, and Montgomerie has also set a new European record for earnings. His impressive playing ability brought him second place at the 1995 PGA Championship and a tie for second place after a gruelling 18-hole playoff in the intense heat of the 1994 US Open at Oakmont. During his college years at Houston Baptist, Montgomerie was a three-time All-American. Winner of the 1985 Scottish Stroke Play and 1987 Scottish Amateur, he went on to be the European Tour's Rookie of the Year in 1988.

1 A most noticeable variance from standard is that Montgomerie plays the ball back in his stance (much like Azinger), but in this case it's linked to a vertical, up and down swing rather than a rounded one and he works the ball from left to right. His right foot is perpendicular to the line which encourages his steep swing plane.

2 At pocket high there's a straight line between his left shoulder and club head, showing the one-piece backswing that generates power through the length and height of the club head's arc. The club head lags behind his hands for the first six inches or so, a sign that he has begun his swing by turning his chest to initiate a takeaway where the chest, shoulders, arms and hands start as a unit. The danger here is that he will turn the club head too much inside as it follows the rotation of his chest. To prevent this, Montgomerie uses a rather weak right-hand grip that allows him to keep the back of his right hand to the sky for a long time during the takeaway. This, along with a straight right arm, ensures that his club is headed up and over him and not back behind him.

3 Montgomerie's right leg straightens to produce the upright swing arc and at the top of his swing his hands are fully cocked with the left wrist cupped, a key move that opens the club face and accounts for his fade. As long as his club face is open he can clear his hips as fast as he wants and he won't hook the ball. Nevertheless, for insurance, he slides his hips just a tad before they clear to prevent closing the club face.

One thing that is very apparent is the length of Montgomerie's backswing. It's longer than most but since it's the result of a large shoulder turn and very supple wrists, it's under control and therefore an asset. Note how straight (not stiff) his left arm is. The club is out of control when backswing length is attained by allowing the left arm to break down. The transition from backswing to downswing is a key part of any swing and it is a characteristic of any star player that they "own" the club at this point in the golf swing.

4 Starting back to the ball his arms drop straight down, a move that's necessary if the club head is to win the race with the body to impact. He is faced with the same problem that all the "up and downers" such as John Daly and Ben Crenshaw have. Since Montgomerie's hands swung so high above him, they have a long way to travel. He gives them the time they need with his lateral hip slide and he doesn't begin to clear his hips until his arms have dropped considerably. This is a different sequence to that of the modern swing in which the hips clear at the same time as the arms drop.

5 **6** Through impact and well into the follow through, Montgomerie's in the Reverse C. This is a result of the fixed axis at the top of his spine that makes his arms sling by him as his upper spine and head rebound away from the target in response to the forces that are acting on his body through impact. Montgomerie is a big man with high hands, a high finish and a lot of talent—he's going to be a star for a long time.

1
2
3
4
5
6

An all-round *athlete*

Ernie Els is probably one of the best all-round athletes playing competitive golf today. With his awesome physical strength, Els can afford the luxury of a smooth and effortless swing. It looks simple because he creates no unnecessary angles with the club shaft.

Ernie Els The modern swing

Ernie Els has conquered the golf world like nobody since Greg Norman. In South Africa in 1992, he became the first player since Gary Player to win the South African Open, South African PGA Championship and the South African Masters in the same year; in 1994 and 1997 he won the US Open Championship; and in Europe from 1994 to 1996, he won three straight World Matchplay titles. In 1999, his PGA Tour win came in the Nissan Open as he claimed his fifth top-20 finish on the Tour.

1 Ernie Els stands very tall over the ball with the bones in the lower leg straight up and down so that the crease of his pants is perpendicular to the ground. This shows that he's bent his upper body forward toward the ball using his hip joints. Straight lower legs also show that he's used his knees, as he should, to incline his lower body backward away from the ball, setting him perfectly in the ready-set-go athletic position which is common to many sports.

Both feet are slightly flared, the right one to allow his sizable body to make a full turn during the backswing, while the left flare grants him the flexibility to turn back through the ball.

2 With long arms and a supple back, his extension away from the ball is enormous and, just as it reaches its fullness, his right wrist begins to fold backward beginning the elevation of the club head. You can see the

1

2

3

amount of stretch he produces by the folds in his shirt. Here he is plugging into the power of coil, setting the top of his body against his lower body.

3 Now all he has to do is fold the right forearm backward as if he were about to throw a ball. His right palm faces the sky anchoring the club in the so-called "tray" position. This is a very solid, no-nonsense position to begin his return swing to the ball. As with many of the modern stars, notice how little his hips have turned at the top of his swing for the length his club head has traveled.

4 To start the downswing, his left shoulder moves away from the chin, dropping his left arm into position. With his left arm parallel to the ground, Els' right foot is still planted but tilting in on the inner rim of his foot preventing any premature spinning of the chest and allowing him to hold his wrist cock until the last second.

5 Just before impact his shoulders are level, and just after impact his right shoulder has risen upward. If his left shoulder were to keep going toward the target his swing center would be pulled forward causing a mis-hit to the right. Note that his hands have returned to their address position and still the club head has not been released. This incredible retention of the angle between his left arm and club shaft is what is termed the "late hit," a poor use of words since there is nothing late about it. This power position is possible because Els (when he is swinging well) never tries to make anything happen—he lets it. His swing unfolds with no untidy edges and the ball just seems to get in the way.

6 His follow through position is, as you would expect, full and fluid, with both arms straight in front of him. This is a position that will bring him to a well-balanced finish.

4

The modern *swing*

The modern rotational swing favors a ball position farther back than the classic swing, and the elegant Elkington is the personification of the modern swing. With his driver the ball is played about even with his armpit. His arms hang comfortably down so if he dropped the club from this position and then relaxed his arms they wouldn't change position. His lower leg is straight up and down with just enough knee flex to give him the most solid balance position from which to make his golf swing. The common mistake—too much knee flex—pitches the body forward during the downswing, an error that causes you to straighten up just before impact to regain your balance.

Steve Elkington The modern swing

Native Australian Steve Elkington spent his college years halfway round the world at the University of Houston where he was a two-time All-American and member of the 1984-85 NCAA Championship Team. Since joining the Tour in 1987, his rock solid golf swing has produced six wins and over four million dollars in earnings. In a dramatic battle for the 1991 Players Championship, Steve bested Fuzzy Zoeller to claim the second most prestigious title of his career. The year 1995 brought a major championship victory when he won the PGA Championship at Riviera Country Club. A spectacular final round 64 forced a playoff and he defeated Colin Montgomerie. This was Elkington's finest season: a repeated victory at the Mercedes Championship, top-10 finishes in the British Open and The Masters, the PGA Championship and the Vardon Trophy for low scoring average (69.62). Elkington must like the PGA Championship; he has finished third in 1996 and 1998, too.

1 At address, Elkington's club shaft, left arm and shoulder form an uninterrupted straight line. He flares both feet about a quarter of a turn to promote the rotational aspect of his swing, making it easier to turn his right hip over his heel on the backswing and to clear his left hip over his heel through impact.

2 His left arm movement starts his swing, setting up a chain of motion that results in a swing where the club shaft is always on the plane angle. There is some left forearm rotation during the backswing, just enough to keep the club shaft on the correct plane angle as his right wrist bends backward to create the 90-degree angle of leverage.

3 The defining element of his swing is the opposition he sets up between his upper and lower body as he moves to the top of his swing. Here he's fully coiled, having set the top of his body against the bottom by using his knees perfectly. His back knee is comfortably flexed and his hips are level. Even at maximum coil his left heel is on the ground and his knee is pointing ever so slightly behind the ball, creating the stretch that pays its dividends in club head speed.

4 Starting down, his left arm slides towards his right foot as his weight shifts to his left hip joint. There's so much down and so much around in every swing and Elkington does the down portion first, slotting the club so that his turn to the ball works for him. Too many golfers in their anxiety to hit, turn their chest (the around) before they do their down. It's an error called over-the-top and, with it, your turn works against you.

About halfway down when his left arm is parallel to the ground, his right knee begins its kick toward the target. Once again you see the simultaneous move of the modern swing where the right elbow gets closer to his body without the right foot unplugging from the ground, while at the same time the left hip turns to the left. Thus the right side resists while the left side pulls, maintaining the opposition and even increasing it just before impact. This is evidenced by the separation of the knees, creating the "straddle" or bandy leg position of the modern rotational player.

5 At impact he's nicely behind the ball. His right heel hasn't flipped up, showing that he has allowed the right side to release but hasn't twisted the right shoulder up and over the ball. He's on his left heel and the outer rim of his foot, indicating a correct weight transfer.

6 As with the rest of his swing, his follow through is perfect. You can see the spikes on his left shoe. His belt buckle faces the target as does his right knee.

The right
grip

There is a tendency in some of the better players, such as Fred Couples, Bernhard Langer and John Daly, to use a strong grip, and it works out quite nicely as long as you resist the temptation to throw your hands at the ball. As a general rule, if you're a handsy player use a neutral to weak grip; and if you're a "body" player with passive hands, use a strong grip.

Paul Azinger The modern swing

In his best ever year on the PGA Tour, 1993, Paul Azinger captured the Memorial Tournament by holing a shot from a bunker on the 18th to defeat his close friend Payne Stewart. He went on to win two more tournaments that year, including the PGA Championship, his first major. The thrill of this spectacular season ended abruptly with a diagnosis of cancer in his right shoulder blade. Azinger dealt with cancer like a true champion, using his illness as a forum to inspire others in their fight against the disease. He returned to the Tour in 1994 and while he has not been a prolific winner since then, he took the 2000 Sony Open in Hawaii.

1 The most notable feature of Azinger's swing is the ultra-strong grip where both the right and left "Vs" point to the right of his back shoulder and the back of the left hand points at the sky. Azinger is fortunate that he has a teacher (the noted John Redman) who recognizes that his grip is not incorrect but in fact is the centerpiece of his success in that it fits perfectly with the rest of his swing parts.

He plays from a narrow stance with well flexed knees and a slightly open body line. As a low-ball hitter he positions the ball well back in his stance, a position that sets his hands ahead of the ball at address, an anti-hook defense.

2 Much of the takeaway is concerned with his left arm as the initiator, synchronizing his upper body turn with very little lower body movement well into the backswing. Note that at waist high the left knee still has not moved behind the ball, a prime characteristic of the modern swing, i.e. a weight transfer but very little lower body motion during the backswing.

3 As he reaches the end of his backswing his back leg straightens somewhat to prevent the club from getting lost behind him (a sure way to hook it), but on the forward swing he reflexes it until both knees are level as his left arm comes parallel to the ground, a position necessary for solid contact with the ball back in his stance.

4 The key to his downswing is his lateral hip movement. Azinger slides his hips forward during the downswing, a move he must make because of his shut club face at the top of his swing. If he simply rotated his hips as he started down, he'd hook the ball off the planet. With his passive hands he keeps the leverage (the angle between his left am and club shaft) intact for a very long time, one of the prime advantages of the modern swing.

5 But his slide stops when it should and just before impact his left hip turns behind him, squaring the club face to the target. This body release gives his swing a quiet look as his arms and chest whirl together to get the job done. As an anti-hook defense, Azinger has very passive hands with hardly any forearm rotation through the ball.

6 Both his arms are very straight long into the follow through maintaining their position in front of his chest. This occurs when you rotate your body correctly through the hitting zone, allowing your right side to keep moving all the way to your finish.

1
2
3
4
5
6

Pavin's
golf swing

Pavin taught himself many years ago to treat his golf swing as a vehicle for getting the ball from one place to another. What does it matter if you arrive in a limousine or a Volkswagen? They're both just vehicles for getting you where you want to go. For Pavin, the golf swing, its technique and its form, is not the centerpiece of the game. Ask anyone who has been taken down by this pit bull of a competitor—Pavin is living proof of the old saying: "It's not how but how many."

Corey Pavin The modern swing

Corey Pavin's 1995 U.S. Open victory at Shinnecock Hills was surely his finest moment in competitive golf. He had been a heavy winner ever since starting on the PGA Tour in 1984, but his 13th Tour win was his first major. Number 14 arrived at Colonial in 1996, but that was his last victory. Known as a shot maker and superb putter, his competitiveness was evident when at 17 he won the World Junior title. Never the longest driver, his game goes up a level in match play as can be seen by his 8–5 record in the Ryder Cup.

Pavin is a feel player. He shapes his shots kinesthetically by sensing how the club should be swung rather than thinking about the technical aspects of getting it done. By doing this he puts his body in some unusual positions and therefore, when he's working the ball, his swing sometimes looks a little odd, but don't be fooled—it's a better golf swing than it looks, as the results show.

1 Pavin sets up wide with heels spread outside his shoulders, giving a stable platform on which to turn. His shoulders are almost level at address, more so than normal. His posture is relaxed with not much spine tilt, preparing him for the flat shoulder turn that characterizes his swing. There is nice spacing between his body and the butt of the club, about a fist-with-the-thumb-extended distance away. His chin is up in the "proud" position, anticipating the arrival of the left shoulder.

Note the perfect 90-degree angle between his lower spine and club shaft as it points to his belt buckle. This maximizes his consistency because a swinging object moves most uniformly when it spins at 90 degrees to its axis.

For the driver, his right foot is drawn back to encourage the draw that gives the length he needs to be competitive. But he can curve the ball both ways depending on the demands of the course, so when he needs to fade the ball he plays from a slightly open stance.

2 During his takeaway Pavin keeps his hands inside the club head until it begins to elevate and open; then he sets the angle about waist high.

3 When his wrists cock, the club head goes higher than the hands for the first time. The left arm is on the toe line and the club head is high and behind him with the shaft through the biceps. Most importantly, with his hands on the toe line, his club head is behind the line giving him the club head depth he needs to match his flat shoulder turn. If he allowed his hands to cross the toe line he'd be so inside that his club head would be trapped behind him. Note his eyes are tracking the ball causing even more tilting of the head as he turns away from the target.

4 At the top, the club face and the shoulder tilt match and if everything uncoils correctly, he'll arrive at impact in good shape. Also, he's maintained the flex in his knees to keep his hips level and, with his right elbow pointing down to the ground, his left arm is on the same plane as his club shaft was at address. This sets the stage for his swing back to the ball.

5 Starting down, the triangle formed by a line connecting his elbows tilts so that the club shaft moves more to the left of the target before it drops downward. This moves the shaft across his right bicep, a perfect on-plane position. Pavin's right heel remains grounded until his hands pass in front of his pants pocket, giving him a stable position to swing through to impact. His hands have returned to the toe line as has the shaft. From here all he needs to do is let the triangle swing his club head to the ball.

6 Note the results of a well-timed release where the club shaft is in a mirror position of frame 2. His head is back with the shaft coming out of his left bicep, showing that he has stayed on the plane angle.

1
2
3
4
5
6

Star *profile*

Brandie Burton began playing golf at the age of nine and throughout her amateur career she collected numerous victories. In addition, she was runner-up at the 1989 US Women's Amateur Championship and qualified for the US Women's Open Championship three times before turning professional. In her year at Arizona State University she was ranked the number one woman collegiate golfer and won six of the seven tournaments on her schedule. Burton turned professional after that year and won Rookie of the Year honors for her eight top ten finishes in 1991. In her third year on Tour, 1993, Burton reached $1 million in earnings in record time and was the LPGA Tour's youngest millionaire ever. That year she won her first major, the du Maurier Classic, and she won this event again in 1998.

Brandie Burton

1 Brandie starts her swing from a solid, balanced position. Since she is broadly built and muscular, she flares both feet out at address to facilitate the turn of her body. Both her left and right hand are in a strong grip position and the ball is farther back in her stance than the standard driver position off the left heel.

2 She starts her motion with a gentle cocking of her wrists followed almost immediately by her left arm and chest turning away from the ball as evidenced by the movement of her shirt logo. Notice her lower body is in an identical position to frame one with her hips still square to the target line. This is the beginning of coil, i.e. turning the top of her body more than the bottom. Though a powerful woman, Brandie is already starting to set the club head up with her wrists to make use of the power of leverage.

3 Her lower body shows marked signs of responding to the motion in her upper body. Her right hip has turned back over her right heel, and her left shoulder has begun to move behind the ball. At this point, she's set the club into a fully leveraged position. Although she's turned her back to the target, her hands are still in front of her chest, pushing the club away, adding width to her swing arc. A common error among amateurs is to get their hands well behind them at this point, a difficult position from which to return the club to the ball.

4 Her lower body has completed its turn back as her shoulders deliver the club to the top of her swing. At the completion of Brandie's backswing her lower body has stabilized and her left shoulder has turned against it and behind the ball. Her powerfully coiled position is evident from the creases in the back of her shirt and the tautness of her left sleeve. Brandie gets the club to the standard parallel to the ground position at the top but, because of her body type and flexibility, she can do so only by bending her left elbow at the top of her swing. Some might call this an error but in a swing this powerful, with the club completely in her control, it's more appropriately named an "individual characteristic." The question is, should you copy it? If you're an elite athlete who practices and plays for a living, and it works for you, then the answer is yes. Otherwise, you'd be wise to concentrate on the more fundamental aspects Brandie beautifully demonstrates.

5 To start her downswing, her right elbow tucks back to her side putting her arms back in front of her body. From the top of her swing she shifted her weight into her left hip and she now begins to turn it powerfully behind her, a move that delivers the club directly to the ball. Though her left hip is turning away from the ball, her head and neck have stayed in their position behind it, creating a reversal of the coil she built in her backswing.

6 At impact she continues the rotation of her body to bring the club to the ball. Though her arms are following the rotation, her head and neck are still firmly planted behind the ball. Here she demonstrates a position common to a good player, but uncommon to a poor player: her left arm, hand, and club shaft are in line with the lower right leg, which shows she's allowed her right side to release. Also, notice her right heel is working to the inside rather than up. When amateurs let their right heel "flip out" toward the target line before impact, it causes their club to cut across the ball. The right foot working in allows the club to be delivered more from the inside so it comes to the ball along the target line rather than across it.

7 Brandie's arms swing past her, literally dragging her up toward her finish position. She's fully released the leverage she built in her backswing as is evident from the recocking of her wrists on her throughswing.

8 Brandie's finish is a result of her right knee "getting friendly" with her left. From the top of her swing to her finish, her left knee was moving away from the right which was chasing it. At the completion of her swing, her ankle, knee, hip, and shoulder joint are stacked one on top of the other, indicating that she has rotated her powerful body fully through the ball.

2
3
4
6
7
8
TOYOTA

Star
profile

In her first year on Tour, Emilee Klein won more money than any other rookie in 1995 and posted two second-place finishes, an appropriate transition from her sensational amateur career. She was the 1988 California Amateur Champion, the 1991 American Junior Golf Association Player of the Year, and was an AJGA First Team All American for four consecutive years. Her other victories included the 1991 US Junior Girls Championship, the 1993 Broadmoor, the 1993 North/South Amateur, and 1993 Amateur of the Year award. During her two-year tenure at Arizona State University she earned All-American status both years, was the 1994 NCAA Champion, and the 1994 Collegiate Player of the Year. In 1996, Emilee got her first two professional victories, including a British Open title, and she finished the year among the top 10 money winners.

Emilee has a unique swing due to her unusual set up position which features a very erect posture. But while it looks unusual, the analysis will show her swing adheres to the basic principles of coil and leverage.

Emilee Klein

1 Emilee is a very accurate player because, due to her set up, she doesn't have a lot of wasted body motion. Neither foot is flared and her knees are pinched in, both of which minimize lower body movement. The back of her left hand faces the target as does the palm of her right hand, a configuration known as a relatively weak grip. Her hands are set in the mid-line of her body, encouraging the more rounded swing arc that is her trademark.

2 Emilee's erect posture causes her to swing the club well away from her and then around her in her backswing with minimal hip turn. In fact, her lower body is so quiet that she appears to have a reverse weight shift, but, by frame 4, you'll see she's well coiled into her right side. She is young and very flexible in her shoulder joints, a condition allowing her maximum arm swing and minimal leg action. This flexibility is only an asset if you can find a way not to over-turn your hips and legs, a problem Emilee has solved nicely with her set up.

3 Emilee has set the leverage for her golf swing, though she does so somewhat later than most players. Her right knee has straightened (though it hasn't locked) and serves as a buttress to receive the transfer of weight so important to her coil. Her left heel has begun to pull off the ground but only in response to her upper body turning behind the ball. In a swing that is known more for its accuracy than its power, perhaps Emilee could benefit by keeping her left heel down to add a bit more coil.

4 Emilee's weight is fully loaded on her right side. Though her left heel has come off the ground, the position of her left knee shows the heel has moved more in than up, a further indication her weight has transferred fully to her right side. True error occurs when amateurs lift their heel up and the left knee juts out toward the target line, indicating their weight has remained on their left side.

5 Coming down, Emilee's hips turn marginally as her right shoulder drops and her left shoulder raises, a move that allows her to swing the club directly to the ball without cutting across it. Through impact her legs act as stabilizers and she gains power by hitting across a braced left leg. Since her left leg is already straight and her right leg is almost straight, she's generating a lot of her force through arm swing and the release of the leverage in her wrists.

6 A further indication of her dominating arm swing is that her shoulders are in virtually the same position in frames 5 and 6, showing a strong hand and arm release. With a weak grip she must have a hand and arm release in order to square the club face. Like all good players, her head is behind the ball through impact and her left hip is moving behind her rather than toward the target.

7 As Emilee swings through, her arms reach maximum extension and then begin to pull her body up into her follow through. Her right forearm has rotated well over her left, further evidence that her swing is geared toward a hand and arm release rather than a body release.

8 The creases in her right shoe indicate that Emilee's follow through is less than full because she doesn't use all of the weight of her body to hit the ball. She is primarily an arms and hands player, which is fine as long as the basics of leverage and coil are satisfied. Emilee has built her golf swing and game around pinpoint accuracy and incredible touch.

2
3
4
6
7
8

Star
profile

Though Juli Inkster is hardly as well known as Tiger Woods, her career began in a similar fashion after she won three consecutive US Amateur Titles. A four-time All-American during her years at San Jose State University, she joined the LPGA Tour in 1983 and captured her first victory in just her fifth event. Julie received Rookie of the Year honors, winning two major championships, the first rookie to accomplish such a feat. Her best year was 1986 when she won four times and posted her career low round of 64 on two occasions. In 1990, she gave birth to her first child and played a limited schedule, but in her next two years on Tour she won twice and earned over half a million dollars. In 1994, her second daughter was born, but she still managed eight top 20 finishes in a limited schedule. As well as winning the US Women's Open in 1999, she has claimed the McDonald's LPGA Championship in both 1999 and 2000.

Juli Inkster

1 Juli addresses the ball with a neutral grip and excellent posture. She plays the ball a little further back in her stance than most players. Unlike Emilee Klein, her feet are flared out with her knees pointing in the same direction as her toes, giving her a solid foundation for her upright swing arc.

2 Like many long-limbed golfers, Juli's takeaway is a one-piece action, with her shoulders, arms, hands, and club all working back and away from her body as a unit rather then around and behind her. In contrast to Brandie Burton and Patty Sheehan, she doesn't fully set the club until she's near the top of her backswing. While there is a lot of arm swing it all occurs as part of coil. Julie does not "pick the club up." She "coils it up" and this is an important distinction.

3 Her lower body has turned away from the target in response to the movement of her long, one-piece takeaway but she hasn't allowed this action to cause her hips to sway, a problem for some amateurs who employ this style (right hip slides laterally outside the right leg instead of turning over the right heel). Julie's lower body has finished its backswing motion and will remain in this position while her upper body continues to turn against it, cranking up her coil. Like many players of this body type, she sets the club very late in her swing, between frames 3 and 4. The danger for golfers who don't have strong arms and hands is that a late set leaves the club in a heavy position because the club head is not underneath the supporting pedestal of the hands. But Juli is strong so she manages her late set beautifully and she keeps the club head in complete control.

4 Though her turn is full, her left foot is firmly planted. Her downswing is initiated by a shifting of her weight from the heel of her right foot to the ball of her left foot, a move that is assisted by the late set of the club. This motion drops her hands and arms down before they come around to the ball.

5 Once the left leg has accepted her weight and her arms have dropped into position, she begins a powerful hip rotation through the ball. Her left hip is turning behind her even though her right knee is driving toward the ball. Also, her right foot is off the ground very early, which is characteristic of players who swing the club in a high arc and approach the ball from a steep angle. She lets her right heel be pulled off the ground in response to the momentum of her swing. Some amateurs push off their right foot which causes a lot of thin shots.

6 Juli fully releases the leverage in her wrists and slings the club past her neck, which is in a rock solid position behind the ball. Throughout her swing, she turns her shoulders perfectly around the axis of her inclined spine. They come level to the ground only after her spine straightens at the finish of her swing.

7 Juli has marvelous extension here with her arms still straight, a result of the velocity of the club moving down the target line. And it is this velocity that pulls her up into her follow through position.

8 Her arms swing through and she finishes in a very upright position with her hands and arms over her shoulders. A beautiful golf swing.

2
3
4
6
7
8
Wilson

Star *profile*

The LPGA Hall of Fame is commonly considered the most difficult achievement in all of sports and only 14 professionals have been able to fulfill its elite entry requirements. Early in 1993, Patty Sheehan reached this lofty goal by winning her thirtieth tournament, and added a fourth major championship to her credit later that year. After an impressive amateur career highlighted by her victory at the 1980 AIAW National Championship, she joined the Tour that same year. She claimed her first victory in 1981 and has won at least once every year since, the only exception being 1987 when she lost a major championship playoff to Betsy King. In 1983 and 1984 she won four tournaments, bettering that achievement in 1990 with five victories and over $700,000 in earnings. Through 1998 Patty won 35 tournaments, including six major championships, the last of which was the 1996 Nabisco Dinah Shore, plus the British Open title. Her earnings are in excess of $5.4 million.

Patty Sheehan

1 Patty's set up features a strong left hand grip, both her feet are flared, and her knees point in the direction of her toes. Her spine is tilted a tad to the right which sets her behind the ball before she even starts her swing. Her arms hang directly downward from her shoulders, indicating that she's bent to the ball from her hips with no hunching of her back. Her left arm is on top of her chest, facilitating an unobstructed arm swing across her chest.

2 In a style typical of the "modern swing," one well suited to Patty's balanced body type, she starts the club back by swinging her left arm across her chest with an early fold of her right elbow and an early set of her wrists. At this point her weight hasn't completely moved to her right heel but it is in the process of doing so.

3 Here her right hip begins to turn over her right heel, and her left knee begins to be pulled behind the ball. She's already created a tremendous amount of coil and she'll increase it as her lower body begins to stabilize and her shoulders and arms continue to turn with her swing.

4 At the top of her backswing, Patty's left arm is swung fully across her chest and has coiled her shoulders behind the ball. Her left foot has been dragged off the ground late in her backswing.

5 Here you can see why Patty has achieved such greatness in her career. She holds her leveraged position, the angle of power, longer than almost anyone who has played the game. The club head is still behind and above her right shoulder but her arms are back in front of her chest and her hands are almost at impact, a fully leveraged position which is reminiscent of Mickey Wright and Ben Hogan. She accomplishes this because her right side holds its position as her left side turns behind her and pulls her arms down. To further assist her in this much sought after position, her left shoulder has moved out from under, and, most importantly, up from under her chin.

6 Notice the triangle formed by her chest and forearms with the shaft of the club bisecting it, an indication of a full and perfectly timed release of her arms, wrists and right side. The beauty of it is that her swing center, located just below her throat, is behind the ball as she delivers her club head, a prerequisite for solid, powerful contact. You can see the force of this momentum continue well into her follow through as the club wraps around her body in frame 8.

7 Patty continues to rotate through the ball with her lower body. She maintains her spine angle for a long time and hangs back just a little bit as both arms extend through the shot. Her left leg is still slightly flexed because she still hasn't fully rotated her hips.

8 She finishes in a perfect follow through position. You'll notice a slight wrinkling in her right shoe, indicating it's holding some weight, but since her follow through is so long and full, this is a recoil from what was a complete release to her left side. Patty's swing would easily qualify for the Golf Swing Hall of Fame, if there was such a thing.

2
3
4
6
7
8

Star *profile*

Caroline Pierce's competitive skill began to show when she reached the semi-final round of the 1979 English Girls Championship and flourished in 1980 and 1981 when she was an English Girls International Champion. At Houston Baptist University, she continued her winning ways, earning All-American honors in 1983 and 1984. After a slow start on the LPGA Tour, she began to build momentum in 1994 with some top ten finishes and almost $85,000 in earnings. She more than doubled her earnings in 1995 with several more top ten finishes and a second place finish at the JAL Big Apple Classic. Caroline earned her first Tour victory here the following year and did so in style. She was the only player in the field to finish under par, winning with a five stroke advantage over a field of top players. The $108,750 prize money helped her finish 1996 ranked 22nd in earnings. Both Emilee Klein and Caroline Pierce stand about five feet five inches tall, with long limbs and slim bodies, so it is no surprise that their swings look similar.

Caroline Pierce

1 Caroline addresses the ball with rather erect posture, which causes her shoulders to turn more level to the ground. The ball is off her left heel, perfectly positioned for a driver. This excellent ball position encourages her square address position, i.e. shoulders, hips, and feet all parallel to her target line, a strong element in her accuracy. Her arms hang comfortably with no hint of tension. Her left foot is flared out at address which helps her build coil as she turns away from the ball, a good idea since her body is the type that turns easily but has difficulty creating coil.

2 If you have a thin frame like Caroline's, you'll need to guard against taking the club too far inside on your takeaway. Her erect posture serves to keeps, her hands moving as they should, back down the line of her toes rather than in behind her as is evident from the fact that her hands and the shaft of the club are still in front of her chest. Her takeaway is a one-piece motion with a very late set of her wrists, the weight of which she controls perfectly in frame 3.

3 The function of Caroline's backswing is to get the mass of her body behind the ball. It is not very long nor does she create maximum coil since her hips have turned almost as much as her shoulders. Though her backswing is short, her hands are in an upright position as a result of her one-piece takeaway.

4 To start her downswing, her hips make a subtle move laterally toward the target while her shoulders remain in a very closed position pointing to the right of target. At this late point in her swing you now see an increase in the tension between upper and lower body, satisfying her need for coil. It's most important to note that, though her hips move toward the target to start her downswing, her head and neck have held their position behind the ball, a prerequisite for powerful contact because it's another element of coil. As she reverses the direction of her club she drops her arms back down, in the complete absence of any hitting impulse by her hands.

5 Once the lateral move of her hips is completed and her weight has transferred to her left leg, she begins to turn her left hip behind her. Caroline's arms, having dropped the club down into a perfect position, are now ready to deliver the club head to the ball.

6 She looks very stable here with her right foot remaining low to the ground. She's hitting against a firm left side, exhibiting the classic impact position of all good players with the back of her left hand facing the target and the club shaft in line with her left arm.

7 Late into her follow through she still has the club shaft pointing at her chest with her elbows in front of her, a sign that she has fully released her right side including her right shoulder. Note how the toe of her left shoe is turned up a tad, showing that her weight is perfectly distributed, starting from the ball of her foot back to her left heel.

8 An elegant finish with her weight fully posted on her left side and the club shaft across her neck. It shows she has held nothing back yet is in complete control. A good finish looks like the player could stay in that pose for a long time and certainly the comfortable and relaxed Caroline sets an excellent example.

2
3
4
6
7
8

Star
profile

In 1995, Barb Thomas had her best year ever on the LPGA Tour, winning the Hawaiian Ladies Open and posting five top 20 finishes. Early in her amateur career she was the Iowa Junior champion in both 1978 and 1979. From there she went on to an impressive collegiate record at Tulsa University where she earned All-American honors in 1980 and posted a convincing third-place finish in the 1982 NCAA Championships. She earned her LPGA Tour card at the first attempt by sinking a bunker shot on the final hole of the qualifying tournament. Barb has improved her swing consistently throughout her career and offers a fine example of strong technique.

Barb Thomas

1 Barb is a very straight driver of the ball due to her excellent set up. The golf ball is perfectly positioned off her left heel and her left arm hangs comfortably atop her chest ready to swing freely. Her feet are straight at address which will serve to increase her coil back and through her golf swing.

2 Barb's arms swing back, creating stretch in her left side, the initial element of her coil. Notice as her arms swing, her shoulders have moved only slightly to accommodate the arm swing and her lower body has maintained its address position. Each of these features adds to her early development of coil.

3 Now her right hip has turned over her right heel, establishing the right side pivot point which will serve as the lower body axis for her backswing. Her left shoulder has turned as it should, around her inclined spine and therefore appears to move downward. Though her arms are still over an extension of her toe line, her wrists have set the club head into a fully leveraged position. In doing so, her hands serve as a pedestal for the weight of the club head as it is elevated to the top of her swing. These are the takeaway characteristics of the modern, body controlled golf swing.

4 At the top of her swing, both feet are planted firmly on the ground. Barb's knees haven't moved much, yet her upper body has fully rotated as shown by the fact that her left shoulder is well behind the ball. To create coil in the modern swing three areas need attention: the shoulders and chest (upper body) turn the most; the hips (middle body) turn the next greatest amount; and the knees (lower body) turn the least. Each level produces opposition, and creating the proper ratios between each produces maximum coil. Should any of these levels turn too much the coil would be reduced and so would the potential for power.

5 Here Barb beautifully illustrates the initial movements that deliver the club back to the ball. You can see how much the club is moving down and therefore why it's called a "downswing." To do this, her left hip has turned over her left heel, yet her right side has held its position to maintain her coil. As a result her hands move downward and away from her right shoulder. Called separation, this downward movement of the hands away from the shoulder slots the club, putting it in a perfect position to take advantage of her shoulder and hip rotation which is about to occur. Now her turn works to her benefit to deliver the club to the ball. Had she turned first and left the club up high, she'd need to struggle near impact to get the club down to the ball and to do so she'd have to stop the powerful rotation of her body.

6 Barb has arrived at impact with her lower body leading the way, but notice how her left hip is turning behind her rather than sliding toward the target. Though her weight shifted laterally from frames 4 to 5, from there she began a powerful rotation of her left hip behind her. A common error among amateurs is to continue the lateral motion and neglect the rotational motion. This puts the body well ahead of the ball at impact and greatly diminishes distance potential. As with all players of her caliber, she arrives at impact with the club back in front of her body, and her left arm firmly planted against her chest to add the power of her body to the hit.

7 With the ball well on its way, this frame shows how well Barb has released her leverage and coil into the shot.

8 Her follow through shows she has delivered her energy to the ball efficiently. Her hips are fully turned, her chest faces left of the target, and she is perfectly balanced on her left foot.

1
2
3
4
5
6
7
8

Chapter five

The long game

The crowning shot of Corey Pavin's 1995 US Open win was his four wood to within six feet of the flag stick, but that shot was set up by his well-placed drive down the right side of the 18th fairway. Whatever Pavin lacks in distance is more than made up for by his precision off the tee.

Ask some golfers how they're playing and they often say: "I'm hitting my woods great but my irons are terrible." Ask them again a week later and the response is: "I'm stiffing my irons but I can't hit my woods". In no other game do we use so many different implements, so it's no surprise that as teaching professionals we hear this all the time. This bouncing back and forth is caused by your brain fixing on one concept about the golf swing and staying with it until, out of desperation, you're forced to change it.

Think of it this way: you sweep the ball off the tee with your woods and hit down on the ball with your irons, and the good players are able to cycle between these two concepts and adjust as they play.

The cycle

Let's take an example to see how the cycle operates. If you're hitting your woods well with the sweeping motion, your tendency is to use that motion on all your shots, with your ball position and stance subconsciously modified to favor your wood swing. And there's no better way to hit tops and fat shots than to swing "up" on a ball that's forward in your stance. When you do it correctly with your medium and short irons, you should hit "down" on a ball that's positioned off your left cheek.

At some point you realize that you're having trouble with your irons so you practice with them or take an iron lesson until your swing is back where it should be and, presto, you start hitting your irons much better. But then your woods go haywire and the cycle keeps running: good woods, bad irons, good irons, bad woods.

To help you avoid this cycle, we have included a special section on woods and irons so that your brain will understand "sweep versus down" and the swing mechanics necessary for both.

Specific *targets*

- **For the route,** always aim at something on the line you want your ball to fly on. It might be a mound, a tree in the background or even a cloud in the sky.
- **For the destination,** pick a tire track or a discolored patch of grass in the section of the fairway from which you want to play your next shot. Once you have the picture of your shot going to a specific target simply focus on making solid contact with the back of the ball.

Your driver

With the possible exception of the long putter, the driver is the longest club in your bag. This means that you'll stand farther from the ball, making your swing more rounded. Your driver does not have much loft so it's usually teed up in such a way as to encourage you to sweep the ball off the tee for optimum launch angle.

Drivers are designed to hit the ball a long way in order to put it in position for your next shot. You probably can't win the hole or the match with your drive but you can certainly lose it if you're in the bushes. Harvey Pennick said that the "woods are full of long drivers" and that's true, but a long hitter named Sam Snead, winner of over 80 tour events, said: "I'd rather hit a seven iron from the rough then a three iron from the fairway." So somewhere between the woods and the rough there's a trade off between distance and direction. You must be long enough off the tee so that your next shot is manageable.

Overswing

Unfortunately, over-swinging with your driver is easy to do. It satisfies many of our natural urges to just whale away at the ball so the tendency is to try to kill your tee ball to get as close to the green as possible. And while it may be natural, this is an urge you must control if your score is important to you—don't be seduced into trying to hit your driver as far as you can.

Pick a route and a destination

How do the good drivers of the ball swing within themselves and put the ball in position for their next shot? They pick a route and a final destination for their driver and so should you.

Our advice is that any time you have a driver in your hand, but especially on wide open golf holes where the urge to blast it is great, choose both a route and a destination, a specific landing area for your tee ball.

Best driver *drill:*

To learn to control your driver swing, tee up two balls side by side. Using your hip speed as the governor, hit the first one at full power and the second at three-quarter power. When you gain control of your swing you'll be able to produce the two different distances almost every time and that will help you on the course to attack with your driver when you need to, and play safe with your driver when you ought to.

The rule *of thumb*

The rule of thumb is to tee your driver so that the top edge of the club head bisects the middle of the ball. If your swing speed is over 95 mph you might consider teeing your ball higher than this. Chi Chi Rodriquez, for many years one of the longest drivers pound for pound, tees his ball well above standard.

Your driver *continued*

1

2

Driver particulars

- On all normal driver shots, tee your ball just outside the left side of your chest about even with your armpit. To make sure that your ball location is correct, lay a club shaft on the ground perpendicular to your ball and touching your left heel.
- If you want to hit your shot higher, to take advantage of the wind at your back or to clear an obstacle, move your ball to the tip of your shoulder but be careful to move it a little closer to you since your club head will be slightly inside the target line at impact as it follows the rounded path of your swing. And make sure you check that your shoulder alignment is square because as your ball moves forward, your shoulders open.
- Note that just because the hole is long, you may not always need a driver off the tee. Tests show that a driver and a three wood of equal shaft length go about the same distance in the air so downwind you might try your three wood for more accuracy.
- Whatever else you do, learn to love your driver. You can bet that the guy who said "drive for show, putt for dough" was already a great driver of the ball. It doesn't help much to knock in a 30 footer for an eight after hitting two balls in the water off the tee.

Best driver tip ever:

When you need your longest drive, take it back extra slow and smooth with feather-light grip pressure.

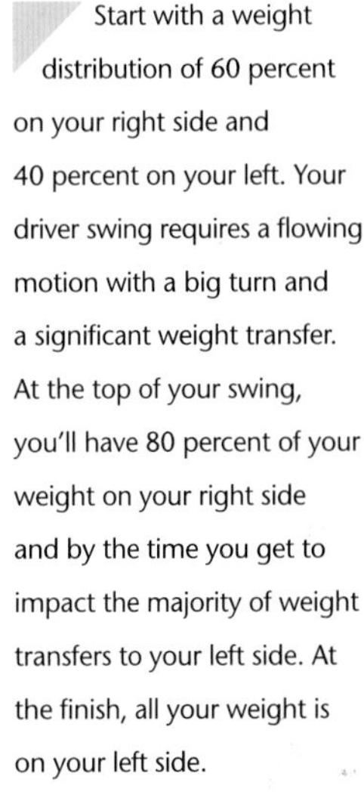

Start with a weight distribution of 60 percent on your right side and 40 percent on your left. Your driver swing requires a flowing motion with a big turn and a significant weight transfer. At the top of your swing, you'll have 80 percent of your weight on your right side and by the time you get to impact the majority of weight transfers to your left side. At the finish, all your weight is on your left side.

Dogleg *tip*

Driving it pretty well except for the doglegs? Instead of changing your swing you could carry three drivers. An open-faced driver puts fade spin on the ball; a closed driver imparts draw spin. So why not use your regular driver for the straight away holes, a four-degree closed driver for doglegs left, and a four-degree open driver for doglegs right? If you decide to try this, enlist a club maker to get the correct specifications.

Your long irons

In our view, the long irons (one, two, three and four) are not for the average golfer. Basically, unless you're an expert, they are hard to hit off the ground because they don't have much loft and the ball must be contacted perfectly to get it airborne.

Just the look of long irons can be intimidating with their small heads, straight faces and long shafts, especially if you are playing the ball as it lies and it is sitting down a little bit. Unless you make solid contact and generate enough club head speed, there won't be much of a difference between your long irons in terms of the distance your ball goes. In our experience, most golfers hit their long irons about the same distance so in actuality you may be carrying three of your four irons in the bag: one marked two, one three and one four. Unless you have a single digit handicap or you're very strong, our advice is to replace your long irons with the four, five and seven woods.

Best long iron *tip ever*

Leave them at home!

Best long iron *drill*

Lay them on the ground as directionals to check your aim and alignment while you practice.

When you hit your irons from the teeing ground, the rules allow you to place the ball on a tee. But be careful not to tee your irons or fairway woods too high in this situation. If you do, you'll make contact high on the club face and hit weak shots with too much loft. The proper teeing height for an iron or lofted wood is just high enough off the ground so that the thin part of a tee can fit between the ball and the grass.

Five-time British Open Champion and the world's most dominant player in his prime, Tom Watson's upright swing gives him the ability to launch high, softly landing long irons that hold on even the slickest greens.

Long irons particulars

Although the long irons aren't for everyone, they can be a good addition to your bag if you can handle them. Since they hit the ball low and long, they're great in the wind when you need to keep the ball down.

If you know the technique and have the talent, you can really maneuver the long irons, bending them around the doglegs and curving them into pins that are tucked to the sides of green. And if you're really strong, there's no reason why you can't hit them high and soft when you have to. That's what the likes of Jack Nicklaus can do, and it's unlikely that you'd find them without their one irons, a great club on narrow driving holes.

The long iron swing

Your long iron swing is much like your driver swing in that it is a sweeping motion but because they are shorter than your driver, your swing will be a bit more upright. Still, you won't take a divot; your goal is to pick the ball off the ground.

■ Play the ball off your left breast. Start with your weight evenly distributed and make a wide backswing, avoiding the urge to pick up the club without turning your back to the target.

■ At the top of your swing, you should have about 75 percent of your weight on your right side with your right hip turned over your right heel. Start down by shifting your weight to your left hip and take care to keep your head from sliding toward the target. Long irons can put demons in your head, the most common of which is fear of hitting the ground before the ball. The "fat" long iron is a feeling you won't forget so, to shallow out your swing, keep your weight shifting and your head behind the ball.

■ About 80 percent of your weight is in your left hip at impact. Finish with your weight completely on your left side and the club over your left shoulder, indicating the fully released right side.

Your fairway woods

The look of your fairway woods is very different from your long irons. When you look down at address, you can see the loft on the face of the club so it registers that getting the ball airborne is not a problem. Moreover, the size of the club head is substantial enough to suggest the forgiveness a large sweet spot offers. What you can't see from address is the sole plate: the bottom surface of your club head which is specifically designed to slide through the grass rather than catch in it.

Even though these features make the fairway woods easier to hit than most long clubs, many golfers don't realize just how important they are to playing good golf. You might not be a good driver of the ball but if you can keep your tee ball in play and then hit a solid fairway wood, it can make up for a lack of distance off the tee.

- Look at your fairway woods as long-range siege guns which will bring you close enough to the green to take advantage of your short game.
- Develop a good short game, combine it with a strong fairway wood game, and you'll be a match for anyone.

Best fairway *wood tip ever*

If they practice at all, most golfers practice their skills separately (driver, putting, chipping, etc.). Develop a "skills package" by practicing with your fairway woods in combination with your pitch shots so that you will be ready to link them when you need them on the golf course. When's the last time that you saw a golfer on the driving range alternating a three wood off the ground with a short pitch to the flag?

Best fairway *wood drill*

1 Tee a ball correctly and hit a shot with your three wood, feeling the sweeping action of your swing.
2 Drop the tee height so that the ball is just barely above the ground, and hit another shot. You should be able to hit both shots without taking a divot.
3 Hit the ball off the ground, again taking no divot. Repeat the sequence at least three times. This three-ball drill will teach you to sweep the ball off the ground with your fairway woods.

3

4

Most golfers play the ball too far forward off their left heel and catch the top of the ball, sending it skimming along the ground. Position your ball off your logo with your weight evenly distributed. Your goal should be to hit the ball with a descending blow that shallows out just before the bottom of your swing arc. It's a full body coil with the same weight transfer as your driver. Think of your fairway wood swing as a sweeping action and let the ball position take care of the "descending" part of your swing. There's no divot.

5

6

Three-quarter *swing*

The need for solid contact is why, beginning with your mid irons, your swing gets tighter and shortens to three quarters. The benchmark to shorten your swing is your left arm. Imagine you are standing inside a large clock with 12 o'clock at your head and 6 o'clock at your feet. You produce the three-quarter swing by stopping your left arm at 10 o'clock. Thus your regular top-of-the-swing position will be between 11 and 12 o'clock. **A note of caution:** As you swing your left arm to its appointed time, make sure to turn your chest along with it.

Best mid iron tip ever: The mid irons are best played with a three-quarter swing regulated by swinging your left arm to 10 on the clock.

Your mid irons

Most architects design their courses so that if you play from the tees that match your skill level, you'll hit a lot of mid-iron (five, six and seven) approach shots into the greens. Thus, in combination with your short irons, your mid irons are your scoring clubs.

The mid irons give you a combination of distance and control because their loft gives you enough backspin to stop the ball on the green. In addition to its height and stopping power, backspin also decreases the amount of hook and slice that you will get with your straighter-faced clubs, such as the driver and long irons. This is the reason why your mid to short irons will not curve as much as your woods and long irons.

A mid iron is best played with a controlled three-quarter motion and even long-swinging John Daly reduces the length of his swing and follow through for the sake of increased accuracy with his mid iron.

The particulars

Because they are shorter than your long irons, you stand closer to your mid irons, and this makes your swing more vertical—another reason why you can make your mid irons "bite" on the greens. To encourage the descending blow, position the ball off your left cheek, just forward of the center of your stance.

At address your weight distribution is 50:50 but since your swing is for accuracy, don't transfer as much weight during your swing as you do with the long clubs. At the top, 70 percent of your weight is on your right side, and by impact the majority of your weight shifts to your left side, where it stays as you rotate up into your finish position.

To be a good mid-iron player you need solid, clean contact with the ball to ensure that you get the distance and direction you expect. When you contact the ball in the center of the club face it won't twist, so the face stays square and the energy in your club head transfers to the ball. Take a shallow divot *after* your contact with the ball to avoid getting grass or sand between your ball and the club face, which would cause the ball to fly off line.

With your mid irons, your stance is slightly narrow. The ball is positioned just forward of the center of your stance, opposite the left side of your face, to encourage a descending angle of attack. Though a three-quarter backswing is most suitable for the mid irons there is still plenty of dynamic motion through the ball and into a full finish.

The *"Chicken Wing"*

In those pressure situations where you absolutely have to hit your ball on the green, the "chicken wing" shot can be a valuable addition to your shot makers arsenal. It's the shot made famous by Lee Trevino and the one Nick Faldo used to win the Open.

Use one more club than normal and aim slightly left. Position the ball in the middle of your stance and take your normal backswing. Drive your right knee toward the target to start your downswing so it leads your hands and arms into impact. Since you don't want the toe of your club to pass over the heel, keep your right wrist bent just as it was at address. If you've retained your wrist angle correctly, you'll finish with your hands in front of your chest and your club face looking at the sky.

The key is to let your left elbow float up and away from your side as you clear your hips through impact. This keeps your club face square to the target line well past impact, assuring a lower than normal shot for accuracy with a left-to-right spin that stops your ball quickly.

Your short irons

Your eight, nine and wedges are the clubs that can turn three shots into two, so pay a lot of attention to them. Again, a three-quarter swing is in order for maximum control. Because the shafts are shorter, you move closer to the ball than with your mid irons, with the ball position between your left cheek and your nose. And, of course, as you would with all your other clubs, you should use the posture outlined in Chapter two.

The particulars

Of all the full-swing clubs, your swing with the short irons is the most compact with the least weight transfer. You start with 50:50, move to 40:60 at the top of your swing, and then to 60:40 at impact. There's no full-bodied movement here.

Good short-iron players have a constant arm speed, minimum hip turn and a grooved rotation rate that delivers the same force to the ball time after time. When you're 120 yards from the green, it's no time for a burst of power resulting in a 145-yard shot.

It's one thing to make a bad swing with the right club but it's often just as ruinous to choose the wrong short iron and make a good swing. Because the value of accuracy rises as you get closer to the hole, you need to choose the correct short iron. However, it is often less simple than it appears because you're in between clubs. It's too far for your normal nine but too short for your eight, and the danger is that worrying about which club to hit will cause you to make a bad swing.

When you are faced with a "tweener", take one less club and hit it harder if you're a strong-swinging, power hitter. If you're a smooth swinger with a syrupy action, take more club and hit it easy. In other words, when you match your club selection to your swing tempo you'll never have to violate your internal metronome, the personal gauge that sets your natural swing pace.

A well-struck short iron starts from a narrow stance and ends in a perfectly balanced finish as shown by Peter Jacobsen.

The knock *down*

The high, spinning wedge that stops after a bounce or two is a plus, but there is an equally useful shot you can play with your short irons: the "knock down" shot. The name is deceptive because you want to hit the ball softly to prevent the force of the blow from driving the ball too high into the air.

- To hit the "knock down" shot, choke down about an inch on your short iron, and play the ball in the center of your stance.
- Set your weight 60:40 favoring your left foot, and keep your weight in your left hip throughout the swing. From this set up you can keep your shot low and under control by using a three-quarter backswing and a matching three-quarter follow through.

With the short irons, take a stance about the width of your hips. Position your ball just slightly forward of the center of your body. Since you'll be most bent over with your short irons, you should be sure to maintain your address posture during your backswing. There is a tendency to straighten up during a short iron backswing and this can turn the high, lofted shot you planned to land next to the hole into a low runner that finds a hazard behind the green.

Best short *iron shot*

To develop the unified upper body rotation (your arms and chest turning at the same rate), hit practice balls with a strap that binds together your upper arms and your chest. Many-times champion Mickey Wright hit thousands of balls with rubber surgical tubing around her arms and chest: a drill that helped her to become one of the most accurate ball strikers of all time.

Chapter six

Awkward lies

Although it is obviously a struggle from such a severe slope, Greg Norman finishes here in balance, a necessary feature of hitting a successful shot from an awkward stance.

The first order of business when you arrive at your golf ball is to examine your lie, i.e. the characteristics of how your ball is sitting in the grass. Your lie dictates the kind of shot you can play, sometimes allowing you to pull off a spectacular shot from 200 yards over a tall tree and at other times preventing you from getting close to the flag from 30 feet. Thus, part of being a skilful player is "reading" the lie and then being able to execute the required shot. We have outlined a variety of lies, ranging from no grass underneath the ball to grass all around it. Each of these situations requires that the club head should sit differently to the ball. The better the lie, the more the club is soled flush to the ground. The more buried the lie, the more your club rests on its heel, requiring you to stand farther from the ball. The tighter the lie, the more the club rests on its toe, so that you stand closer to the ball.

Difficult lies around the green

Tight lies

When there's little or no grass under your ball the first order of business is to determine exactly what is under the ball. Is it sandy soil, thin grass with dirt or the difficult hard pan lie? Each is played from a different set up that changes the length, path and timing of your swing.

From a thin lie

You're near the green with not much grass under your ball and what little there is, is patchy. In this situation, choose your sand or pitching wedge to give you the proper amount of loft you need to stop your ball on the green.

If your set up is right, you're well on your way to solving this difficult lie. The danger is that you'll hit behind the ball, snagging your club head in the ground. To guard against this, place your weight in your left hip and stand closer to the ball with a more upright spine position. This makes your club shaft more vertical and automatically tips your club head onto its toe, reducing the bounce of the club. This way, less of your club head is exposed to the ground. Your upright posture also causes you to raise your hands at address, protecting your wrists from over-cocking.

Since the heel of your club is off the ground, position the ball toward the toe of your club where you'll want to make contact. Striking the ball on the toe is not only safer but the slightly off-center hit produces a much softer shot. Once you're set up correctly, your swing is the same as it is for a normal pitch shot.

Difficult lies around the green *continued*

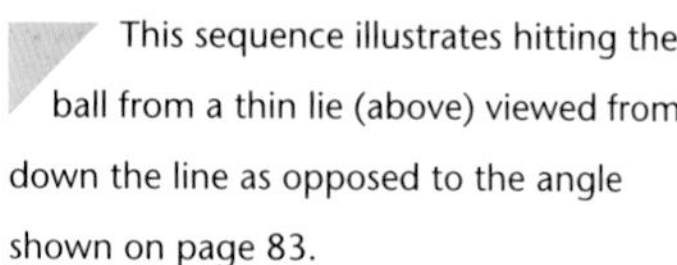

This sequence illustrates hitting the ball from a thin lie (above) viewed from down the line as opposed to the angle shown on page 83.

From hard pan

When your ball comes to rest on a patch of rock-hard ground with no grass to prop it up, the last thing you want is your club head bouncing into the center of the ball and causing a skulled shot that runs out of control.

To play this type of lie correctly, select a sand or pitching wedge and position the ball according to the trajectory you need:

- Forward for a high soft shot.
- Center for a standard pitch.
- Back for a low, running pitch.

As with the thin lie, move close enough to the ball so the club head is standing on its toe with the club shaft as vertical as possible. Thus you eliminate any angle in your left wrist, making sure that your club head won't drop any lower through impact than it was at address.

Set your feet according to the length of the shot you intend to play: wide and square for a longer shot, and progressively more open and narrow the shorter you want to hit the ball. To shorten the distance your shot flies, open your stance by dropping your left foot back from the target line with your club face slightly to the right of the target. For the swing, use your pitching action.

Buried in grass

When your ball is buried in the grass, your club head should rest on its heel, with the toe of the club off the ground, just the opposite of the hard pan set up. By setting the club on the heel, the bounce of the club is increased along with the potential hitting surface. This increased surface area helps your club head plow through the grass, helping you make solid contact.

When you stand farther from the ball your hands hang lower, presetting your wrists, and creating a steeper angle of attack so that the grass behind the ball has less effect on the shot. Also, by lowering your hands, your shoulders tilt more as they swing, producing a more upright backswing that adds to the cutting action of your swing—just what you need to carve your ball out of the grass. When your club is on its heel, be sure to position the ball in the middle of the club face to avoid any possibility of a shank.

The deep grass tends to grab the neck of your club, twisting your club face into a closed position at impact. This causes a pulled shot left of target so aim to the right to compensate for the pull. And of course you have to swing harder than you normally would with a firmer grip pressure that helps you retain control of your club, as it encounters the resistance of the grass.

Summary

The lie of your ball determines the set up necessary for each circumstance. An easy way to remember it is: if your lie is tight, think "up tight" (hands up for a tight lie). If your lie is buried, think "low down" (hands low for a buried lie). The amount you adjust your club on its toe or heel is determined by how tight or buried the lie is. The tighter the lie, the higher the hands; the more surrounded your ball is by grass, the lower your hands.

Strategy from *sandy soil*

Blast or pick?

The sandiness of the soil is the determining factor for this awkward lie. You can play this shot like a regular sand shot where you deliberately hit the sand first or you can treat it as a pitch shot and catch the ball cleanly. It's often hard to determine the consistency of the turf under your ball: the rules don't allow you to improve your lie and so it's dangerous to poke around. The safe way is to check the surrounding area at least one club length from your ball and if there are any sandy spots similar to the one you're on, test one of them to evaluate the soil texture. If you find the sand is fluffy and powdery don't hesitate to play an explosion shot.

If there's not much sand or you're not sure what's under your ball, it's better to pick it cleanly with a pitch shot than explode your ball with a sand shot. If you make a mistake with the blast shot and there's hard turf underneath, you might end up farther away from the target than you started, whereas a missed pitch falls just short of your target.

Your putting *stroke*

In the types of awkward lies outlined here, the common themes are that the most accurate golfing stroke is one that is as level as possible to the ground, and that a major cause of inaccurate shot making occurs when your club swings vertically upward, opening the club face and imparting side spin to your ball. The problem with side spin is that you're never sure whether your ball will release (keep rolling) or trickle to a stop. Thus side spin is the enemy of roll and you should do what you can to keep your club head low.

Difficult lies around the green *continued*

The wood chip

When your ball lies just off the green and there's no obstacle between you and the pin that prevents you from rolling the ball, the play is a fairway wood. A seven wood is an excellent choice as it has enough loft to lift the ball out of grassy lies and its long shaft allows you a compact swing that's low to the ground. If you don't carry a seven wood you can adapt your other fairway woods by simply opening the club face a tad and moving the ball a little more forward in your stance.

To chip with a wood, use either your putting or full swing grip, assume a slightly open stance and tilt the shaft of your club until it's upright. You'll have to stand erect to accommodate the length of the shaft but be careful to keep your weight anchored on your left side so you don't sway as you make your stroke.

Now use your putting stroke, keeping the right wrist angle formed at address throughout the swing to avoid a wristy stroke. Let your club head swing through the hitting zone as an extension of your arms so it "chases" the ball to the target.

The collar shot

Every once in a while your ball stops against the first cut of rough just off the green. It's hard to judge this shot because using a normal chip or pitch, you're denied clean contact with the ball due to the intervening grass. A three wood adapted like a chipping iron is an excellent choice in this situation. The weight and mass of your three wood head ensures that the club slides through the grass to contact the ball crisply. As in chipping, raise your three wood on its toe, close the face and grip down on it with your putting grip. Assume a narrow, open stance and stroke the ball as you would a putt of equal distance. Expect your ball to hop a little and then roll to the hole like a putt.

Another solution is to choose a putter and address the ball so that the toe of your putter aims at the top of the ball. The key to this shot is to strike the ball squarely with a firm tapping stroke, keeping the toe going at the hole during the follow through.

You can also play this shot by striking the middle of the ball with the leading edge of your sand wedge. This way your club face never touches the ball so you don't have to worry about the grass getting between your club face and ball. To "belly" the ball so that it rolls with a good deal of top spin, use your putting motion with absolutely no wrist action. Just set your weight on your left side and hover the edge of your sand wedge behind the equator of the ball, then make a smooth stroke.

When your ball is just off the green, ignore the markings on your clubs and play the shot with the club that gets the job done. Your goal is to keep the ball on the ground whenever you can, so you might choose a fairway wood, a five iron, a sand wedge or a putter to get the ball close to the hole.

Full swings from awkward lies

When you face an awkward lie some distance from the green, put your course management skills on high alert. Many times you'll have to "play it safe" rather than trying a shot from 200 yards off an awkward lie. But when the rewards outweigh the risks involved and you know the proper technique, you can go for the green with confidence.

From a tight lie

Once you judge the lie to be "tight", i.e. sitting with very little grass under it, everything in your set up and swing is designed to make sure you pick the ball cleanly. It's a little bit easier to hit a short shot from a tight lie but a full swing requires attention to two additional elements: weight shift and shot shape.

Since your left hip is the turning axis of your swing, your weight shift is minimal but your turn is not restricted. You want to pick the ball off the turf or even hit it slightly thin, so your swing is an upper body one, mostly an arms and shoulders effort. For this reason, take at least one club more than normal. Remember that you're going to fade the ball with your club face slightly open at address and this costs you some distance, but it's worth it because the open club face at impact helps get your ball airborne. To encourage the fade, move the ball forward in your stance and draw your left foot back a bit.

From heavy rough

When you find your ball in deep rough you have to make two critical evaluations: "What score do I need to make?" and "How will the grass affect my swing?" If you're playing match play and your opponent is next to the pin with a sure par, the shot you'll choose is different from one if it was the second hole of a 36-hole medal play tournament. Obviously, the shot you choose depends on the circumstances and the extent to which the ball is buried in the grass.

Below: to win the 1987 US Open Scott Simpson needed a whole arsenal of specialty shots, not the least of which was the technique to power through the knee-deep rough without the club face slamming shut.

Pine *needles*

We've chosen pine needles to discuss the awkward lie where your ball sits off the firm ground, on a mat of leaves, twigs, etc. A good practice is not to ground your club, a precaution that avoids a penalty shot should your ball be dislodged as you take your stance.

For this shot, hover your club head over the ball, open your stance and, with your weight firmly planted on your left side, pick the ball off the needle carpet. To do this, position the ball in the middle of your feet. The shorter the shot, the shorter your backswing and the less your weight shift. Around the green, it's mostly an arm swing with the firm, wristless hand action of a chip.

For a full shot you need a good shoulder turn along with your normal wrist cock but your weight stays in your left hip joint. This way you can coil your upper body around your spine without your feet slipping and sliding about. The trajectory is likely to be a low one so adjust your plan accordingly. As in the fairway bunker, think "thin before fat", a cue to pick the ball without hitting the ground first.

Full swings from awkward lies *continued*

There are some lies from heavy rough where all you can do is take your sand wedge and hack the ball back to the fairway. It depends on the thickness and texture of the grass. Even though it doesn't appear to be as thick as some of the American grasses, the tall, wild version of fescue found in some seaside countries, such as Great Britain, is tough to play out of. It is strong in texture with enough spacing between the shoots for a ball to settle down at the base of the blades, defying extraction to all but the strongest swinger. In tropical climates, you'll often find Bermuda grass in the rough and, while it is neither as long nor as visually impressive as the tall, waving fescue, it is a gnarly grass that can smother your club head.

The bottom line is that you should know what kind of grass you are up against and adjust your shot plan accordingly. When you play a course for the first time, ask the pro or the superintendent about the grasses. And at your home course, practice out of every kind of rough you can find to see what effect it has on the distance and direction of your shot.

One thing for certain is that heavy grass, no matter what type, will rap around the neck of your club, shutting the face and producing a low pulled shot to the left of target. The harder you swing the more this effect is magnified so the distance that your shot has to carry affects how much to the right you should aim to adjust for the pull: the longer the shot, the farther right you must aim. Obviously, you can't tell for sure how much pull to allow for, so, if there's trouble on the right, it may not be prudent to aim it there. The same goes for trouble on the left. Greg Norman was fooled on the 18th hole in the final round at Doral in 1995, when in close competition with Nick Faldo. The gnarly rough closed his club face and he pulled a six iron 40 yards into the lake to lose the tournament.

Lies that are harder than they look

Most lies are obvious in their degree of difficulty; a buried lie in the bunker, a steep sidehill lie or a ball half submerged in the water gets your undivided attention. But there are some lies that appear so benign there's a tendency to ignore the important effect that they have on your ball's flight.

Grass against

In this situation, the grass is growing in the opposite direction to your club head as it swings into the ball. The danger is that you'll catch some grass before the ball, slowing down the club head and causing your shot to come up short. In addition, the grass is liable to wrap itself around the neck of your club so that the ball squirts to the left.

The key to this lie is to make a steeper swing than usual to avoid the grass and hit the ball first. To do this, play the ball in the middle of your stance or even a little back of center. Take at least one club more, open your stance and grip the club very firmly.

To cut through the grass, your club head must approach the ball from a steep angle. To produce a steep path, move the ball back in your stance. To further steepen your swing and create the proper angle of attack, settle your weight into your left hip and leave it there while you swing. Grip down on the club with a firm hold in preparation for the control you'll need at impact. Hover the club above the ball so you can make a smooth takeaway without getting your club caught in the grass. At impact you'll need to hold your club face open as the grass pulls on the neck of your club, so let your left elbow finish horizontal to the ground with your right palm facing the sky.

As we saw with the buried lie, one of the hardest aspects of the grass against shot is aiming. The longer and more gnarly the rough, the more you must aim to the right of target, and it's hard to convince yourself to do this even though you know that you should.

Grass with

When the grass grows in the same direction as your downswing it acts as a launching pad so you can expect a flyer—a shot that goes farther than normal and won't stop well once it hits the green.

Play the ball slightly more forward in your stance than you would normally and take at least one less club (say, a six rather than a five). Open both your stance and the face of your club and make a smooth swing with a proper weight shift.

The last thing you want is to hit a pop-up by making an upright "all arms—no weight shift"

Full swings from awkward lies *continued*

swing that drives the club head into the grass before it gets to the ball. Just concentrate on making solid contact with a full follow through and let the grass be your friend.

The perched lie

This lie props the ball up as if it were on a tee. However, it isn't on a tee and the danger here is that you'll swing right under the ball and hit a weak shot that goes nowhere. Since the ball is an inch or two above your feet, if you take your normal swing, your club comes at the ball on a steep angle so you contact it much too high on the club face.

To prevent this there are several alterations you should make to your set up. Pull your right foot back from the line of flight and make sure that your left shoulder points slightly right of the target. This closed position encourages a more rounded swing arc that neutralizes the natural tendency toward steepness, but don't forget to aim to the right of your target to allow for the closed stance.

Move the ball forward in your stance. If you normally play this shot in the middle, move the ball opposite the logo on your shirt. If you would normally play it off the logo, reposition it off your left heel. And always choose at least one less club—you should move from a six to a seven.

The last adjustment is crucial. Hover your club head behind the ball without letting it touch the ground. There are two reasons for this. Firstly, when you sole your club head behind the ball, you run the risk of pressing down the grass and

To keep your club head from sliding under a perched lie, hover it above the ball.

Although it looks inviting, the perched lie can be dangerous without the proper adjustments.

dislodging your ball. And if your ball moves in this situation, it's a penalty. If you don't sole your club, you are deemed, under the rules, not to have taken your address position and there is no penalty if your ball changes position.

Secondly, hovering your club face directly behind the back of your ball gives you a better chance of making square contact at impact. You want contact with the back of the ball rather than the ground, so that's where you aim your club face.

Out of a divot

Hitting into a divot may be a bad break but recovery is not as difficult as most club golfers expect. Depending on the position of the ball in the divot, there are different shots you can play that require different techniques. If your ball lies in the front of the divot, your goal is to sweep it out with your regular swing. If it's

near the back lip of the divot, you modify your swing and punch it out. Regardless of where the ball lies in the divot, always stand closer to your ball. This sets the club shaft more upright, reducing the chance that your club head will catch the edge of the divot.

Sweep the ball from the front

It may look like a troublesome shot, but when your ball is in the front of the divot with nothing between your club face and the back of the ball, you can take your normal swing. The only modifications are in your set up.

Always sweep the ball from the front of a divot.

Move the ball about an inch forward of where you would normally position it in your stance. This allows you to sweep the ball cleanly, using the divot to direct the path of your club. If the divot is deep and points left of the target, open your club face to produce a fade back to the target, then swing down the divot line. If the divot points right of the target, close your club face slightly to promote a draw back to the target and simply let your swing path follow the divot line.

Out of a divot
green side

If you're around the green and your ball is in a divot, simply use your chipping stroke with a high lofted club. However, if there's a steep front lip to the divot and the pin is at the back of the green with no hazards in your way, it may seem strange, but the shot here is a "topped putter." You'll want to hit the top of the ball so that your ball caroms off the lip of the divot, pops up into the air and hits the green with an abundance of over spin that carries it to the flag.

Move the ball opposite your right toe so your hands are markedly ahead of it. This creates an abrupt down stroke that pinches the back of the ball, causing it to pop up immediately. Hover your putter head behind the ball, even with the top third and simply make an arm and shoulder stroke with no independent wrist action.

The tendency when using a putter from a divot is to use too much force when all you need is a smooth stroke not much harder than normal for a putt from this distance. Hit a few practice shots using the "top spin putter" shot, and get a feel for how much force you need.

Full swings from awkward lies *continued*

Punch the ball from the back

When your ball trickles into a divot and rests at the edge of the back lip, you have to dig it out so plan for a low, running shot. Play the ball one inch behind the center of your stance and choose one club more than normal. Choke down about one inch and swing abruptly down on the back of the ball using an abbreviated follow through. Use a mid to short iron and don't be afraid to turn on the power for this one.

If the ball is lying at the back of a divot, always punch it out.

Your ball comes out of a divot low and running so aim slightly to the right of your target. And don't challenge the architect if he's put trouble in your way, especially if there's water between you and the target. Remember that the goal from this lie is to get your ball into a good position for the next shot.

1

2

3

4

5

6

Shot from shallow water

If your ball lands in a temporary accumulation of water it's called casual water and under the rules you're entitled to a free drop on drier ground. But when your ball is in a water hazard it costs you a penalty stroke unless you exercise your option to play your ball as it lies.

When you knock your ball in a water hazard, most of the time it's too far below the surface of the water to play it. But, occasionally, when it just trickles down the bank of the hazard, you'll find it half submerged and it's possible to have a go at it.

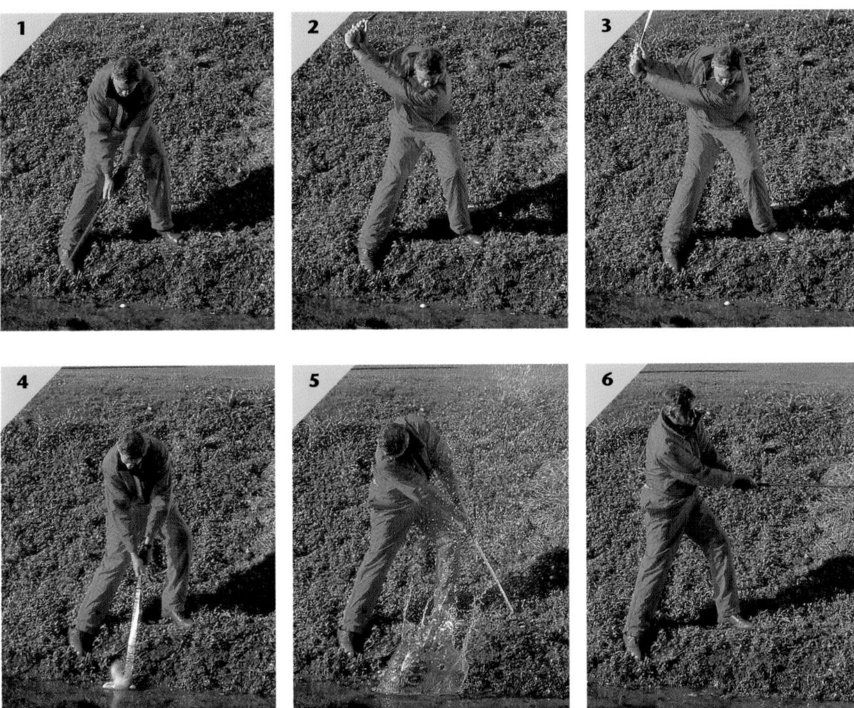

If the ball is more than half submerged, don't try this shot but once you decide to play the ball out of the water, here's how. Take a wide stance for stability. The last thing you want is to lose your balance from this awkward position. Your swing is primarily an upper body motion, mostly an arm and chest swing with very little weight transfer. Play the ball in the middle of your stance and hit down behind it, taking as little water as you can. Your follow through should be shorter than normal, and you must take care not to move your head in anticipation of a face full of water.

Risk versus *reward*

The first consideration is how you stand in your round. Is it time to take a chance or do you need to play conservatively and take a drop? The second is how far you can expect to advance the ball. If hitting the ball out of the hazard can gain you only a few yards, opt for the drop. If you can hit your ball out of the water two or three clubs (20 to 30 yards) closer to the green, it might be worth the risk.

Uneven lies

The right *clubs*

Unless it's a very subtle slope, an uneven lie is no place for a long iron or fairway wood. The distance may require your three wood but your course management skills should tell you to play a safety shot back to level land and let your short game save your par. It would be a very unusual instance for the average golf player to use more than a five iron from a severe slope.

People who don't play golf often wonder why golfers make such a fuss over the difficulty of their sport. But it doesn't take long for the beginner to realize that golf's not just another stick and ball game. Uneven lies are one of many examples where, without the proper technique, a simple swing at the ball won't do. Golf has been called the game of a lifetime and in one sense it is because it can take a lifetime to master all the skills required to play it. Once you do, you'll find that golf isn't quite as difficult as you thought, though it's never as easy as the non-golfer suspects.

A precarious stance

Course designers build in swales, grass-filled depressions, bunkers and mounding around the course to present new challenges to your inventiveness as well as your balance. And since your body seeks to stay in balance even at the expense of your golf swing, a precarious stance can be very disruptive. When you're perched on the bank of a bunker or halfway up a mound, it's no place for a big weight shift and a lot of body motion—it's more of an upper body swing dominated by your wrists, arms and shoulders.

Maintaining your balance from an uneven lie has to be your number one priority, although sometimes it's almost impossible.

Maintaining your balance

The first priority when you have a precarious stance is to maintain your balance. Take your set up and after you've stabilized your lower body by anchoring your feet into the hill, swing your club head over the ball to determine the effect of your body motion on your balance. Make your practice swings identical to the real swing you are about to make, except that your club head swings over the ball instead of actually hitting it. Once you're ready, let your swing be guided by one thought—you must keep your knee flex constant throughout your swing. The tendency from a precarious stance is to either increase your knee flex and hit the ball fat or straighten your knees and hit a low, bladed shot.

Ball above or below feet

Almost all the shots you hit on the driving range are from lies where the ball is at the same level as your feet. Thus your brain learns the geometry of making a level swing and adjusts your balance system accordingly. But if you've played any golf at all, you know that there are situations on the course where the ball is either above or below your feet and if you don't make the necessary adjustments, uneven lies can cause some bad shots. The trick is to understand the effects of the lie, set up to it correctly and make as close to a normal swing as possible.

Characteristics of uneven lies

Properly executing shots from uneven lies is a challenge for all golfers. In order to play effectively from these types of lies, you must first develop an understanding of the effects they have on your swing. There are four basic types of uneven lies:

1 Ball above your feet.
2 Ball below your feet.
3 Downhill.
4 Uphill.

For each of these there is a predictable ball flight pattern and simple adjustments that you can make to your set up to compensate for the effect the slope has on your body. The gravitational forces of the hill will challenge your ability to make a balanced swing, and although we'll show you how to adjust your set up to compensate for the pull of gravity, you will be much more successful if you concentrate on making a three-quarter swing motion from these uneven lies.

Effects of uneven lies

1 The ball follows the angle of the slope.
2 The loft of the club face points in the direction of the slope.
3 You'll lose your balance down the slope.
4 The bottom of your swing arc is altered by the slope.
5 The path and plane of your swing are altered by the slope.

General adjustments

Although uneven lies tend to be opposites of each other, there are general adjustments that are standard for all of them. In every instance, make it a priority to protect your balance by anchoring yourself into the hill against the pull of gravity. Angle your shoulders to match the slope so that you can swing with the contour of the hill. The slope causes changes in your swing arc and you need to adjust your ball position accordingly. And, finally, by opening or closing your stance, you neutralize the effect of the slope by returning your hips to level.

Once you've made the correct adjustments in your set up, you need to do only two things: the first is to make a smooth, three-quarter swing for maximum control; and the second is to focus on the target.

Uneven lies *continued*

Ball above stance

When the ball rests above your feet, you're forced to swing flatter, more around your body, causing your shot to fly to the left of target usually with a right to left spin. When it's above your feet, the tendency is to pull or hook the ball, and to offset this there are several modifications you can make.

When the ball is above your feet, it tends to fly to the left of target.

Since all good swings depend on balance the first order of business is to neutralize the tendency to be pulled down the hill. Flex your knees into the hill for balance with your weight forward toward the balls of your feet, and leave it there as you swing. Also, be sure to keep your weight on the inside of your right foot. The danger is that as your swing progresses, the momentum of your turn will topple you backwards down the hill, an error you can prevent if you are well anchored on your right side.

Take one club more and choke down so that you can stand closer to the ball. Move the ball back in your stance because you'll reach the bottom of your arc sooner when the ball is above your feet. To account for the tendency to pull the shot, allow your shoulders to close, an alignment that will aim your club face to the right of the target. With both your shoulders and your club face aimed to the right, your swing takes an in-to-out path that offsets the tendency for the ball to start left. Once you have aimed properly, simply swing the club, allowing your set up to determine your swing path.

Summary

1 Sole the club to establish your posture and the plane of your swing.
2 Grip down on the club.
3 Move the ball back in your stance from where you would normally position it for a level lie.
4 Stand more upright with knees flexed into hill.
5 Make a three-quarter motion concentrating on keeping your balance throughout the swing.

1

2

3

4

5

Ball below stance

When the ball is below your feet, your swing is more upright so your club face tends to point to the right of the target at impact, curving your shot from left to right. If you don't make a correction, your shot is likely to fly low and right.

Prior to arranging your feet, sole your club flush with the slope, so the shaft is more upright than normal. This establishes your swing plane and your posture at address. The upright position puts the club on its toe and aims the club face right. Since the ball is farther from you, the bottom of your arc occurs later in your swing, so to catch the ball solidly and give your club face time to square up, move the ball forward in your stance. This points your shoulders left, offsetting the tendency for the ball to start right of your target.

When the ball is below your feet, it is actually farther away from you, so stand closer, with a wider stance and more knee flex to lower yourself to the ball. Pinch your knees in and turn your feet in to minimize side-to-side motion. Settle your weight onto your heels and into the hillside to further anchor your lower body. Because the hill pulls you forward onto your toes as you swing back to the ball, you need to stay on your heels from start to finish.

Summary

1 Sole the club to establish both your swing plane and posture.
2 Stand closer to the ball.
3 Move the ball forward in your stance from where you would normally position it for a level lie.
4 Widen your stance, pigeon toe your feet and flex your knees into the hill.
5 Make a three-quarter motion concentrating on keeping your balance throughout the swing.

When the ball is below your stance, it tends to fly right of target.

1

2

3

4

5

Downhill and *uphill lies*

To adjust your body to accommodate the slope, visualize trying to balance a table on a slope. In order to keep it from tipping you must shorten the uphill legs to make it level. When your ball is on a slope in golf, you do the same with your uphill leg to create a level hip turn.

For downhill slopes, draw your right foot back away from the target line and increase the amount of flex in your right leg. Do the opposite for an uphill slope. Since it is your shoulders that dictate both the path and tilt of your swing, the next step is to angle them to match the slope of the hill, allowing your swing to follow the natural contour of the incline.

The amount you open or close your stance depends on the severity of the slope. For both uphill and downhill slopes, you should adjust your stance until your hips are level. For both types of lie, the ball is played in the middle of your stance.

Uneven lies *continued*

1

Uphill lies

On an uphill lie, your ball is higher than your right foot but lower than your left. The slope acts as a launching pad, adding height to your shot along with a tendency for your ball to go to the left. When you sole your club, the effective loft is increased because of the slope. For these reasons it's best to take more club from an uphill lie.

On an upslope, your left foot is drawn back from the target line, effectively shortening your left leg and leveling your hips. With your left foot dropped back, your weight settles comfortably into the hillside as an anchor for balance. Flare your left foot out to make it easier to get through the shot. Since you want to swing up the slope (not into it), tilt your shoulders to mimic the slope of the hill, with your left shoulder higher than your right shoulder.

In the case of a severe uphill slope, it's important to level your hips as much as possible, but when you do, you change the low point of your swing. When you open your stance, the ball in effect moves back, and when you tilt your shoulders to match the hill, the bottom of your arc moves forward. The two adjustments match perfectly when your ball is played from the middle of your stance. Your swing from an uphill lie is upper body dominated and it's important to let your arm swing follow the slope of the hill so that you finish with your hands high and behind your left ear. Once you reach this point, the momentum of your arm swing pulls you backward down the hill and you shouldn't try to stop it.

Summary
Uphill lies

1 Open your stance until your hips are level.

2 Flare your left foot.

3 Tilt your shoulders to match the slope, your right shoulder lower than the left.

4 Position the ball in the middle of your stance

5 Make a three-quarter swing and just concentrate on keeping your balance throughout the swing.

With your left foot drawn back from the target line the hips are now almost level, which helps the golfer keep his balance on a difficult slope. You can see that he has not allowed his open stance to open his shoulders; they are square to his target and angled with the slope.

Uneven lies *continued*

Downhill lies

The technique for dealing with the downhill lie is exactly the opposite of that of the uphill lie. On a downhill lie, the ball is below your right foot and above your left, making it difficult to transfer your weight up the slope to your right side during your backswing. It's also hard to stay behind the ball on the downswing when the hill is pulling you forward toward the target.

To compensate for these difficulties, use less club (you might use a six iron instead of a five) and choke down to reduce the distance you hit your shot. Aim to the left of the target and draw your right foot back until you level your hips. This not only provides you with stability but squares your shoulders to the target line.

Tilt your shoulders so they match the slope of the hill and position the ball in the middle of your stance to place it at the bottom of your arc. Your left foot should be toed in to prevent you from sliding down the slope.

With your weight firmly anchored in your left hip, make a good upper body turn away from the ball using your left hip as the axis all the way through your swing. The major error here is to try to lift the ball into the air, a sure way to top it, so take special care to swing down the hill, letting your club head follow the contour of the slope.

On a steep downhill slope, you'll often see tour players who look as though they are walking after the ball on their follow through. That's because they swing down the slope with their club head and step over their left leg as they "walk through" the shot. They haven't lost their balance as many observers think; they've maintained it by letting the walk through happen.

You should expect a low, running shot from this downhill lie.

Summary

1 Choose a more lofted club and choke down on it.
2 Move the ball to the middle of your stance.
3 Tilt your shoulders to match the slope, left shoulder lower than right.
4 Close your stance to level your hips.
5 Make a three-quarter motion concentrating on keeping your balance throughout the swing.

1

2

3

4

Chapter seven

Shot making

When you think about it, most of the golf you play is a deviation from the norm. You may hit only five regulation irons in a round of golf, while the rest, depending on your talent level, will be improvised shots, some higher than the norm to clear an obstacle, others curved on purpose to get to a protected target and still others bumped along the ground with no regard whatever for the aesthetics of the shot.

The golf course itself is a place specially designed to take us away from the norm. With its mounds, bunkers, wind and weather, it demands adjustments to the spin and trajectory of your shots. When you can make these adjustments on demand and in the proper context, you are demonstrating the art of golf—and what a true pleasure it is to be able to do this.

For the draw, your right forearm and hand are on top of your left with your right hand knuckles to the sky, indicating a full release of the hands and arms through the hitting zone with the toe of the club rotating over the heel. The club is tilted away from the target line with the club head pointing well left of the target.

To be a complete player you should know how to control the trajectory of your ball as well as how to draw and fade it (it's called "working the ball"), but even if you have not arrived at this level yet, understanding what causes your ball to spin left and right, stay low or fly high, will make you a better player and help you understand what is happening in your swing when your ball flight takes on these characteristics.

Why you need to work the ball

Usually for regular play and always for tournaments, pin placements are rotated from hole to hole so as not to favor a particular ball flight. There are some cups set toward the front of the green, some in the middle and back of the green, and some to the sides both left and right.

Off the tee there will be some straight holes, some that bend to the right and some that bend to the left.

Obviously if you can't curve the ball, they can "hide" a certain percentage of the pins from you and you'll be going against a certain percentage of the doglegs. If you hit your shots from right to left, it's hard to get at pins which are tucked on the right edge of the green because it is dangerous to bring your shot in over the hazards that guard the greens. If all you can do is move the ball from left to right, the left pins are tough to get at, but when you can curve the ball both ways as well as control its trajectory you can get at any pin no matter how hidden it is.

The strategy for a full shot

For full swing shots, working the ball can be used to negotiate pins tucked behind bunkers and water hazards. Rather than aiming straight at the flag, and running the risk of landing in trouble with a pull or a push, aim at the center of the green, and configure your set up to move the ball toward the flag.

If your shot shape is correct, you'll knock it close; if you hit it straight, you're in the middle of the green and even if you pull your shot, the worst that you will have is a lag putt from the other side of the green.

When the flag is in the back of the green, aim for the middle of the green and bring your shot in low so it can run to the flag. When the flag is in the front of the green, aim for the center and bring your shot in high so it will either spin back to the pin or stay where it lands, giving you an achievable putt for your next shot.

For the fade, Els uses left hand control with very little forearm rotation at impact.

Three *drivers*

If you're like most golfers you can't curve the ball on command. But there is one trick that you could add to your bag that will help negotiate the doglegs, and the good news is that it has nothing to do with changing your golf swing. All you need do is to carry three drivers. All else being equal, the more open the face of your driver the more left-to-right spin you'll put on the ball; the more closed, the more draw or hook spin. So to get the spin you want, use your regular driver for the straight away holes, a four-degree closed driver for dogleg left holes and a four-degree open driver for the dogleg right holes. Enlist the help of a club maker to get the correct specifications and do remember the 14-club limit if you are playing by the golf rules.

Most importantly, before you go on-course take your new weapons to the practice tee and make sure you do two things: imagine the curve of every shot before you swing and ensure you make your regular swing letting the club face rather than conscious manipulation do the curving for you.

Imagine
your shot

Your mental image of the shot is of equal importance to the planning and technique of curving the ball. Images cue motor behavior and the more vivid and complete your image is, the more precise the cue. Great players use imagery for every shot. Chi Chi Rodriguez, a premier shot maker, explains that he "paints the portrait" of every shot in his mind before he hits it. Sam Snead, when asked how he curved the ball, said, "I just think fade or draw." Jack Nicklaus claims that he "goes to the movies" before every shot and sees the shot exactly as it should be before he swings. Seve Ballesteros and Greg Norman do much the same.

Thus rather than being paralyzed by too many swing thoughts, the great players cue up their muscles with the correct thoughts, and in no segment of the game is this more important than in the creative part of the game known as "working the ball."

The importance of the follow through

While it is important to image your swing as a whole (see it, feel it and even hear it), you should pay special attention to your follow through. While you never consciously try to curve the shot with your swing, you do need to have a very clear concept in your mind of your finish position before you swing (see the chart on page 109). For the draw finish, your club shaft points to the left of target; for the fade it points to the right. When you want a high shot, image a high finish; to keep your shot low, image a low finish.

The concept

The number one rule is that you work the ball with your set up and your follow through—not by manipulating your golf swing. First make the image of your shot, then take a practice swing which is a perfect rehearsal of the swing you want to make, focusing on your follow through.

As we've seen, what you think about your swing influences how you actually do it. If you want to fade the ball, set up for a fade and program your mind so that your swing is "on the way to a fade finish." Then, free from any in-swing manipulations, let your swing benefit from the geometry you established at address between your body, the club, the ball and your target, and simply swing through to the appropriate finish position. The same holds true for all the other specialty shots, including the draw and the high and low shots.

Shot making requires a variation from this perfectly "square" address geometry.

There are three lines you will use at address.

- **The target line**, a straight line from the target through your ball.
- The second is your **shoulder line**, a straight line connecting your shoulders.
- The third is the **intended line of flight**, a curved line that includes the line on which your ball starts its flight.

Adjust the ball position for the shot shape (see page 109) and aim your club face directly at the target using the target line as your guide. Without changing your club face aim, adjust your shoulders to the shape of the shot. Open shoulders for high, fading shots; closed for low, drawing shots. Check your grip pressure and swing down your shoulder line so your finish matches your shot shape.

The fade

To fade the ball, align your body to the left of the target with your club face pointing at the target. For your normal shots, your shoulders are parallel to the target line but for the fade they should be open, ensuring that when you swing on your shoulder line, your ball will start to the left of the target.

After starting left, your ball curves back to the target line due to an open club face at impact. This puts cut spin on your ball providing the curve you need to bend your shot. Remember that even though your club face is square to the target at address, it is open to your intended line of flight at impact. Your finish shows the effects of quiet hands and good body rotation through impact with your club shaft angled to the sky or even tilted toward the target line for maximum curve.

The draw

For the draw, everything is just the opposite of the fade. Aim your club face along the target line with your shoulders pointing right of the target in a closed position, parallel with your intended line of start.

From this set up if you make your normal swing along your shoulder line, your club face will be slightly closed at impact causing a soft draw that curves from right to left back to the target. Your finish reflects a fully released club head with it pointing left of the target.

Should you have to hit a major league slice or a hook, make only two additional adjustments. To hook the ball, instead of aiming your club face at the target, point it slightly to the left and close your shoulders more. For a slice, aim the club face to the right and open your shoulders more. With these simple adjustments you will magnify the amount of side spin you put on your ball.

The high shot

There are times when you have to hit the ball higher than you normally do. You might need to stop the ball softly on a hard putting surface or you might decide to take advantage of the wind behind you to hit an extra long drive. Most commonly, you will want the valuable high shot in your arsenal to loft your ball over obstacles such as trees or water.

As with the draw and fade, proper execution involves two elements: your image of the shot and the actual technique of setting up and finishing correctly.

1

2

3

4

5

6

The image

For the high shot, picture your ball soaring over a tree back into the safety of the fairway. Feel the fullness of the motion in a practice swing. Hold your follow through a fraction longer to feel the high handed finish.

Finish high to hit it high

The key to this shot is a smooth swing followed by a full follow through with your hands well above your shoulders. But don't try for a longer backswing or you'll change your swing timing.

Move the ball forward about one ball width and tilt your upper body toward your back foot, feeling as if your right ear is over your right knee. With a short iron, be sure to aim straight at the target because it is tough to fade a short iron; otherwise aim to the left of your target expecting a fade. It's a dangerous shot because the ball is so far forward in your stance, making it easy to slide your body toward the target, so be sure to keep your spine stationary and turn your shoulders around it.

There's also a danger that in attempting to hit it high, you'll try to lift the ball into the air with your swing using only your arms and hands. Unfortunately, with no weight transfer your club will plow into the ground behind the ball, leaving it well short of target. Make a full chest turn away from the ball, without any lifting motion, then let the loft of your club face do its job to create the trajectory you want.

The low shot

When circumstances, such as wind or a low-hanging branch, force you to keep the ball low, the knock-down shot is the shot of choice. It produces what we call "soft distance", meaning that while the trajectory is that of a fast-moving, hard-to-stop long iron, the knock down actually comes into the target softly with some stopping power.

Play the ball one inch back of its normal position and choke down on the club. When you move the ball back, your club face and shoulders automatically align to the right of the target so open your stance to realign your shoulders to the target. This also moves your weight to your left side, and helps to reduce your backswing producing more control.

The swing itself is simply a three-quarter motion with the weight remaining on the left side throughout the entire motion. However, be sure to turn your left shoulder behind the ball or you'll slap at it with too steep a return swing, producing a higher shot than intended.

1

2

3

4

5

6

The image

To keep the ball low with control make the opposite modifications to those used for the high shot. Image the low trajectory you need as you make a practice swing that is safe and rhythmic. Avoid any images of chopping or punching. Then select two clubs more than you normally would but choke down on the club handle about two inches.

Finish low for the low shot

The general keys for the low shot lie in your swing rhythm and follow through. Most golfers hit the ball much too hard in this situation and the force of the blow drives the ball up in the air. Swing smoothly and finish with your hands, elbows and club head below your shoulders.

Grip pressures

These differ depending on the shot. Your hands control the club face, and how tightly you hold the club and the distribution of the pressure in both hands determines which hand has control at what point in your swing. Knowing how to adjust your grip pressure to match the type of shot you need is a major part of being able to work the ball.

- **For a slice:** tighten your hold on the club in both hands but increase it the most in your left hand so you can pull your club through impact. Anytime you start your downswing by pulling toward the target with your left hand, you'll leave the club face open at impact, causing your ball to spin from left to right.

On a scale of one to ten, if your normal pressure is a three, ratchet your fade pressure up to a four in your right hand and a six in your left. The increased firmness in your hands discourages wrist action (cocking/un-cocking), and the more stiff-wristed your swing, the more likely you are to produce a fade.

- **For a draw:** gear back to a two on your grip pressure index and loosen your left hand grip down to one. This will activate your wrists, giving them the flexibility to work the club face into a slightly closed position through the hitting zone, thereby resulting in a draw that moves away from the trouble.
- **For a high shot:** relax the pressure in both hands and create an "oily" feeling in your wrists.
- **To punch the ball low**, especially if the lie is bad, increase the grip pressure in both hands so that the club won't turn in your hands on contact.

SET UP	FADE	DRAW
BALL POSITION	Driver: opposite left toe	Driver: one ball-width back from left heel
	Irons: opposite left heel	Irons: two ball-widths back from left heel
FOOT POSITION	Open: left heel 2" farther from target line than right, left foot flared out at 45-degree angle	Closed: right heel 2" farther from target line, left foot flared out 20 degrees
SHOULDER POSITION	Same as foot line	Same as foot line
CLUB FACE	Aimed at target	Aimed at target
GRIP PRESSURE	Firm with last three fingers of left hand; wrists fluid	Very soft with last three fingers of left hand; wrists fluid
SWING	Down shoulder / foot line	Down shoulder / foot line
FOLLOW-THROUGH	Club tilted toward target line	Club tilted away from target line
SWING IMAGES	Lee Trevino, Bruce Lietzke	Fuzzy Zoeller, Gary Player

SET UP	HIGH	LOW
BALL POSITION	Forward one ball width	Back one ball width
FOOT POSITION	Open	Closed
SHOULDER	Open	Closed
GRIP PRESSURE	Light / fluid wrists	Tight / firm wrists
FOLLOW THROUGH	High elbows and club head; club shaft body behind	Low elbows and club head; club shaft in front of body
IMAGE	Hitting into a cloud	Hitting under a tree limb

The long runner

Since the long runner spends a good deal of time on the ground, it is best played on a course with firm fairways and light rough so its roll won't be interrupted. Practice this shot on the driving range to get a feel for the amount of roll and learn to play it on your home course first, where you are familiar with the conditions.

When the surface of the green is hard, dry and unreceptive to even a well-struck iron, try the long runner if conditions permit.

When there's no obstacle, such as a bunker or water, blocking your access to the pin, the low running shot merits consideration. It has often been said that the European tour players have this shot in their bag whereas, except for a few US Tour players like Lee Trevino and Tom Watson, most Americans don't. The low runner can be played from many distances and under windy conditions it is almost essential.

You can figure that your shot will fly about half of the distance to your target in the air and roll on the ground for the other half. There is very little force exerted to hit this shot, with the club head speed coming from your body rotation and the unforced swinging of your arms.

To get the feel of the low runner, choose a mid-iron with the ball in the middle of your stance and pick a spot where you want your ball to land. Visualize it running from there to the pin and then take a practice swing that mimics the slowly paced two-quarter backswing you want for your actual swing. The end of your backswing comes when your left arm is parallel with the ground, and when you finish your swing it's your right arm that is parallel to the ground. In between, all you do is rotate back and through with no "hit" at impact.

You will notice that your right forearm has passed over your left, fully releasing your club head through impact. This action causes the toe end of your club to rotate counter-clockwise, imparting a slight right-to-left spin. The fact that you applied minimum force to the ball keeps it low, and because you've set your wrists, your ball has enough backspin to keep it airborne for half of its journey.

Right: The perfect release for the long runner

Caution

The long runner is a good shot to know but before you try it, make sure that it's not wet or sandy in the area where your ball will be on the ground. The other condition to check out is the direction and thickness of the grass in front of the green. If it's against you and a little shaggy, it will be too tough to judge the roll so opt for a shot with a higher trajectory that carries over the problem area.

The bump and run

When you're playing to an elevated green with minimum room between the pin and the edge of the green, instead of trying to loft the ball to the pin, you may have to use the bump and run if you want to get your shot close to the flag.

Move the ball back in your stance for the bump and run.

The technique

Position the ball about an inch back of center and use a seven iron, placing your hands ahead of the ball so the butt of the club is about even with the inside of your left thigh. Keep your weight on your target foot throughout and reduce your wrist action to almost zero, making your swing mostly with your arms and shoulders. Your goal is to hit the ball into the hill with a low trajectory that causes it to bounce upward, slowing its pace just enough so that it runs forward onto the green.

Granted that it's a tricky shot to judge but when you have to get your ball close under these conditions, it is the bump and run that should be the shot of your choice.

Use minimal wrist action to increase the accuracy of this shot.

1

2

3

4

5

6

The lob shot

The lob is last in the sequence of shot options that runs: "Putt it first, if you can't putt it, chip it, if you can't chip it, pitch it and only when conditions eliminate all of the others do you lob it." But even though the lob shot is the hardest of the short shots to judge, there are some situations where you have to play a high, ultra-soft shot to get to your target.

You can use this pitching technique from around the green when you want your ball to go up in the air for most of its flight so that it clears the trouble (bunkers, rough etc.), lands softly, and settles next to the pin with not much run. The lob requires a full-body motion much the same as your regular swing except that you cut way back on the power.

The shoulder line

There is often confusion when the golfer is instructed to swing down the shoulder line from an open stance. As your shoulders rotate, your club rotates with them so that your club is always swinging on your shoulder line. In a misguided effort to follow this advice, many golfers simply take the club away on their shoulder line but fail to turn their shoulders. This forces them to chop down on the ball in a cut across motion. Or they snatch the club inside the shoulder line too quickly and force it to the outside on the downswing. Either way you are sure to shank the ball.

The lob *continued*

The loop

1 The key to the softness of the lob is that your power comes from the length of the arc. Your club head moves to the outside of the target line during the backswing, then back to the inside on the downswing on a looping path. When you swing your club back on your toe line, using mostly your arms, your club head will move to the outside of the target line because your body, including your feet, is aligned open to the target.

2 As you near the top of your swing, the momentum of your arm swing pulls your left shoulder toward the ball, rerouting your club head back toward your body so it can approach the ball on the shoulder line during the downswing.

1

2

The lob shot technique

The image word for the lob is "syrupy" and your concept of the shot should be "full motion with minimum power." The key is to make a silky, flowing swing, moving the club face with the rotation of your body, with no manipulation by your arms or hands.

Since your body leads the way throughout your swing, your club head stays trapped behind you and is still open at impact exposing the bounce on the bottom of your sand wedge. Thus your club head has no other choice but to slide softly under the ball as you swing to a full finish.

Use a sand wedge or, if you carry one (and you should), a lob wedge. Aim your club face slightly to the right of your target to put both height and stopping spin on the ball. Position your hands even with your golf ball at address and play the ball off your left heel with the majority of your weight on your left side, distributed about 80:20. Once your club face is in position, align your body a bit left of the target to allow for a tad of left-to-right spin toward the hole. For increased height and spin, open your stance more and swing more aggressively down your shoulder line.

Remember this shot calls for a long, lazy swing so you don't have to concentrate on cocking your wrists—just relax your wrists and momentum will give you just the right amount of wrist set.

During your backswing, keep your weight in your left hip joint as your upper body rotates away from the target. On the downswing, the rotation of your body is led by your right knee as it leads your club head to the ball.

Your left shoulder moves toward the ball to some degree, i.e. your chest turns and your shoulders close relative to the target. Therefore to swing the club correctly on your shoulder line, your club must follow your shoulders as they turn during your backswing.

This is why your set up is so important. Your shoulders must be aligned left of the target (open) with your club face pointing at the target. This way your ball will start slightly left of the target with a soft, left-to-right spin.

"Long to long"

Your high arm swing results in a high finish emphasizing the fact that you are actually swinging your club from "long to long" when you hit the lob shot. A common mistake is to swing the club using a long backswing and a short, decelerated follow through. This "long to short" action either dumps the ball in the hazard you were trying to carry or you skull the ball over the green.

Because it's such a short shot your brain rebels at the idea of such a long swing—this is one reason why many golfers make a short, quick swing that ruins the shot. With this type of pitch the idea is to control the distance of your shot by the speed of your body turn, rotating both your upper and lower body at the same "easy does it" rate. To get your brain used to the timing of the shot, hit bunches of high, soft pitches on the driving range. Once you add this shot to your arsenal don't forget to hit a few before every round that you play.

Chapter eight

Pitching

Two-time Major winner Payne Stewart shows a compact pitching motion with quiet hands, which are the key ingredients for a stylish, well-executed pitch.

The pitch differs from the chip shot in that it requires more air time than ground time. While the chip is a stroke similar to the putt with no lower body action, the normal pitch is a swing, much like your full swing. The keys to good pitch shots are:

1 To set up correctly.

2 To allow the adjustments in your set up to dictate the shape and length of your swing.

3 To make a smooth rotating swing, which allows you to swing down your shoulder line.

The four absolutes for pitching

The first absolute

Your club face always points at the target

At address your club face must always point at the target. Note that there's a difference between body *alignment* and club face *aim* when the terms open and closed are used. For example, when your shoulders are open they point left of target, but when your club face is open, it points to the right of target. In this case, if your club face were pointing in the same direction as your shoulders (to the left of target), you'd pull your shot.

There are times in pitching when you need to either open or close your shoulder alignment and, since shoulder alignment affects club face aim, you should check your club face to make sure it's correct. When you open your shoulders your club face points to the left of target (closed) and for your pitch shot to go straight you need to adjust the club face until it points directly at the target. When your shoulders are closed, your club face points to the right of target (open) and you should close it until it looks directly at the target. It's only when your shoulders are parallel to the target line that your club face needs no adjustment because it already points at the target.

The second absolute

The butt of the club points at the center line of your body

At address the butt of the club should point toward the center line of your body. With the underhanded throwing motion of the pitch, the only way you can contact the ball on the center of your club face is to position your hands in the middle of your body so that your club face "beats" the neck of your club to the ball. By keeping the butt of the club pointing at the center line, the effective hitting area of your club face is increased.

At address, the butt of the club points to the center of your body.

Unfortunately, too many golfers set their hands well ahead of the ball at address, unintentionally taking loft of the club face and losing the height they need for their pitch. Hands ahead also cause other problems with your pitch shots. They cause your club face to sit on its leading edge, making it impossible to use the bounce of your sand wedge correctly to slide under the ball.

You also run the risk of the necked shot because the neck of your club head is positioned ahead of the club face at address, "exposing" the hosel so that even a small error causes the dreaded shank.

Distance
control factors

The distance you hit each shot is determined by three adjustments to your address position:

1 The length of the club (how much you grip down on it).

2 The width of your stance.

3 The openness of your stance.

How you arrange your body at address will determine how far you can comfortably swing the club back and through in balance and it is this motion that modifies the distance your ball travels.

The four absolutes for pitching *continued*

1

2

The third absolute

The swing is of equal distance back and through

How far you swing the club back determines how far you swing it through. The length of your backswing and throughswing should be a mirror image of each other. Maintaining the same length on both sides of the ball keeps you from adding any extra hit to it through impact. Acceleration of your club head takes place naturally due to the leverage created during your backswing and this combines with the effects of gravity and centrifugal force, give you the club head speed you need. That's why good pitchers of the ball look so smooth as the club swings back and through; they don't seem to "do" anything except get results.

What you don't see is the exercise of leverage supplying the power for a matching arm swing on both sides of the ball. Any time you try to add or subtract speed during your swing your balance is disrupted, making it hard to square your club face to the target at impact.

The fourth absolute

The club swings along your shoulder line

Your club should always swing along your shoulder line. Your body is designed so that, unless you prevent them, your arms follow the route taken by your shoulders as they rotate and, since your hands hold the club and are attached to your arms, the chain of movement that controls the club face is dominated by your shoulders.

When your shoulders swing to the left of target so will your club. When your shoulders are square to the target, your club swings down the target line, and when your shoulders are closed, the path of your club is to the right of the target line. On a normal pitch shot, with the ball in the middle of your stance, your shoulders should be parallel to the target line, regardless of the length of the shot. As you move the ball forward for a higher trajectory, your shoulders open, promoting an out-to-in club head path. As the ball moves back in your stance for the low shot, your shoulders point to the right of target, ensuring an in-to-out club head path.

An underhand throwing motion

When you throw a ball a short distance, your stance is narrow, with your hips facing the target. Your throwing motion is upper-body oriented with your arm swing in control generating the distance. As you need to throw the ball farther, the positioning of your body adjusts automatically to accommodate the length and velocity of your arm swing. These are the same distance principles that apply to the pitch shot.

Narrow, open and gripped down

The shorter the shot, the closer your feet are to one another. Any time you narrow your stance, your swing becomes restricted and more upper-body oriented, and this shortens the distance your ball flies. You should also open your stance to reduce the length of your backswing.

In addition to a narrow open stance, you shorten the distance of your pitch shot by choking down on the handle of your club.

Summary

To be a good pitcher of the ball apply no conscious "hit" to the ball. The pitch is made with a smooth swing, the force of which comes from the constant acceleration of your club head due to the length and leverage of your backswing. And the best way to control the length of your backswing is to make the following three key adjustments: change the length of the club by gripping down on it, open and then narrow your stance.

Thus, assuming that you don't over swing, a narrow, extremely open-foot configuration produces a very short shot. As you widen your stance and make it less open, you increase the length of your backswing, producing a longer shot.

Trajectory control

The trajectory is controlled by three factors:

1 The force of the blow to the ball.

2 Ball position.

3 The squareness of your club face at address.

How hard you hit the ball is determined by the length of your swing, with no attempt to create distance through manipulation of your hands and arms. The longer your swing, the faster your club head moves through impact, increasing the height of your shot.

The farther forward (toward your left foot) that you position the ball in your stance, the higher and softer the shot will fly. The farther back you position the ball, the lower and more rolling the shot will be. So to hit a high soft shot you must position the ball forward in your stance; to hit normal shots the ball should be positioned in the center of your stance; and to produce low, running shots, you move the ball back in your stance.

Opening your club face increases the loft and bounce of the club, producing high trajectories. Closing your club face has the opposite effect.

1 For a higher trajectory, move the ball forward in your stance and open your club face.

2 For a lower shot, position the ball back in your stance and close your club face.

Choosing the right trajectory

To choose the trajectory you need for your shot, analyze the relationship between the amount of fairway or rough you must fly the ball over versus the distance between the edge of the green and the hole. If the area you need to fly the ball over is less than the amount of green you have to work with, then your shot should be low and running.

If the area you need to fly the ball over is greater than the amount of green you have to work with, then the shot is more lofted. If they're about equal, your shot selection is a standard pitch.

Always choose the least lofted shot possible because a rolling ball is easier to judge.

Trajectories

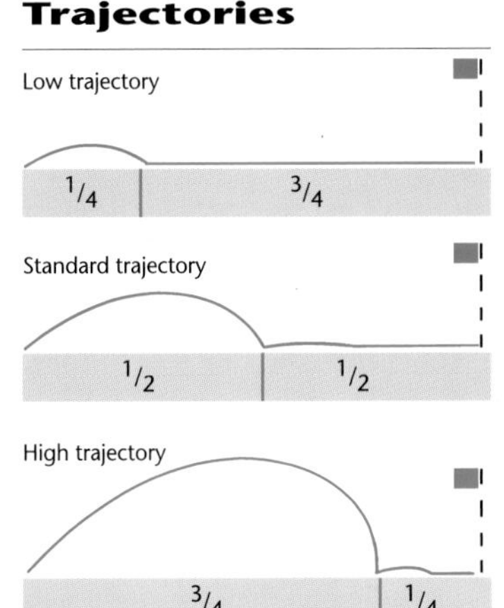

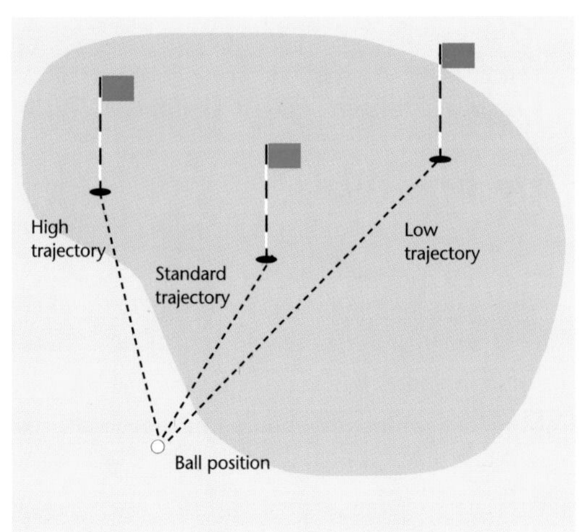

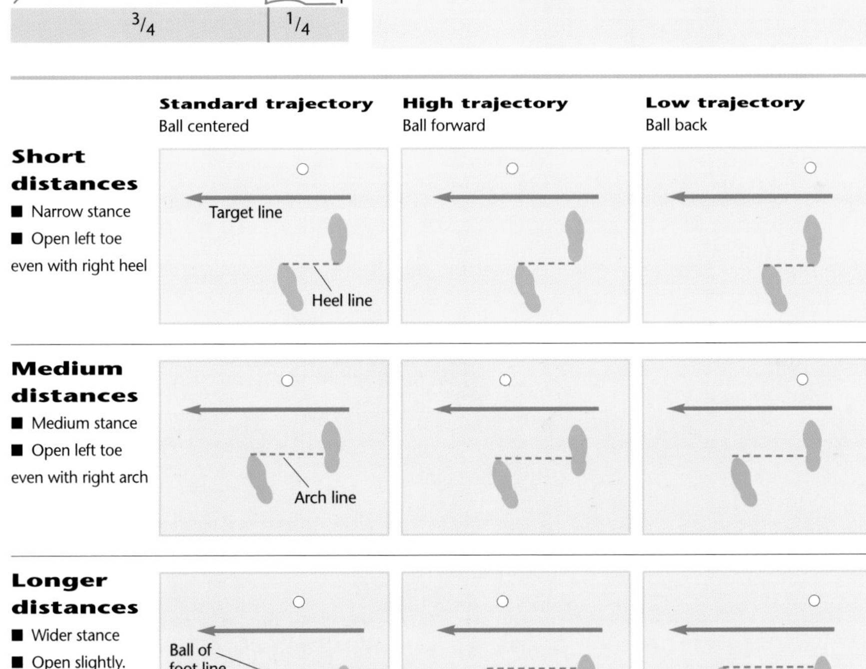

The right *arm*

For the high soft shot, the right arm folds during your takeaway, opening the club face. For the run shot, your right arm remains straight on the takeaway, hooding and closing the club face.

The pitching technique

Since you can't pick where your ball lands when you miss the green, you can count on having to hit a high soft shot over a bunker, or some other obstacle, at least once or twice a round. It's true that all good players miss greens; it's also true that they are decent if not excellent pitchers of the ball.

Grip pressure

For maximum control of your pitch shots we advocate using your normal full swing grip. The palm of your right hand should face in the direction in which you want to hit the ball. The back of your left hand points in the same direction as the club face. Your left-hand grip is firm enough for control but not so firm as to induce muscle tension in your wrists and forearms. The grip pressure in your right hand should vary with the length of the shot.

On short shots, where you swing the club back to waist high, take a firm grip with both hands. This curtails wrist action and without the wrist lever you'll hit shorter shots. For longer pitch shots, your right-hand grip pressure should be light to allow a longer swing with more wrist cock.

Setting the leverage for your pitch

For the short pitch, your hands never rise above waist high. For the medium-length pitch, they stay in the middle of your chest about logo high. For the full pitch, they swing to about shoulder high. The key is that while your hands and arms stay low, your club head is elevated above your shoulders by the setting (cocking) of your wrists. This gives you the club head height you need for sufficient backswing length but keeps your arms and hands under control.

Weight shift and rotation

For all your pitch shots where your stance is narrower than hip width, your weight stays in your left hip joint as you swing. But don't just stand there on your left foot and swing your arms up and down as if you were chopping wood. Take care to rotate around your left hip axis as you swing the club.

For long pitches you'll have a good deal of rotation; for short ones, hardly any at all. The short shot is primarily an arm swing to waist high but when the shot is longer your shoulders are included. As the shot continues to increase in length, the final power source, the hips, become the focal point of your swing and a weight shift from hip to hip takes place as your hands swing to shoulder high.

Once you have created the ideal posture and set up position, you are ready to swing the club back. To become a proficient pitcher of the ball, avoid overusing your hands. For the normal pitch shot, your hips and upper body turn the club away from the ball, while your lower body delivers the club back to the ball.

While we write of weight shift as if it were something you should think about while you swing, it most definitely is not. Shifting your weight from hip to hip is merely a response to your arm swing and upper body turn. It is correct to describe weight as being *pulled* by momentum from one hip to the other, but do not try to do it while you swing.

The swing

The triangle formed by your shoulders and arms remains intact until waist high with the butt of your club pointing at your navel. There is no wrist cock until the weight of your swinging club head creates a natural hinging of your wrists. Only when your right elbow begins to fold do your wrists hinge.

Your lower body initiates the return of your club head to the ball by rotating your left hip and knee back through the address position. This keeps you hitting down and through the ball. Never allow the club head to pass your hands through impact.

The most common mistake made in pitching is to stop the arms abruptly at impact in an attempt to put a "hit" on the ball. When this happens your left wrist collapses, sending the club head past your hands in a flipping action that makes solid contact impossible. You can avoid being a "flipper" by keeping your arms moving well into your follow through. To do this effectively, you must keep your left hip rotating as you swing through the ball.

Allow your coil to dictate the amount of swing produced, with your hands finishing at the same height as they were at the top of your swing. This way, the length of your swing will always match the length of the shot: in other words, a short swing for a short shot, and a long swing for a long shot. Thus you will see that your backswing and follow through actually are a mirror image of each other.

Quiet, then *active*

Good pitchers of the ball have minimal leg action during the backswing while their upper body creates the length and leverage necessary for the shot. During the forward swing, however, there's a good deal of leg action with the right knee moving aggressively to the target. This "quiet-then-active" sequence is often reversed by the poor pitcher so that the lower body (hips and legs) are very active on the backswing but dead during the forward swing leaving the hands and arms to over-manipulate the club.

Chapter nine

Chipping

Tom Watson's low club head and firm left wrist throughout the stroke are keys to good chipping.

Even the best pros in the world miss on average about six greens a round yet they manage to shoot par or better, so it's obvious that how you handle the close shots from just off the green plays a major role in how well you score. Here's the rule of thumb for these sometimes awkward little shots. Ask yourself two questions: first "Should I use my putter?" and "If not, can I use my putting stroke with another club?"

Obviously you shouldn't use your putter when the conditions are against you, e.g. if the grass through which your ball must roll is too long or if there is a hazard in the way. That's a judgment call and your scores will reflect the quality of your decision. However, if you can roll the ball smoothly, without having to take too big a backswing with your putter, do so. The reasons for this guideline are two-fold. Firstly, it's easier to judge the distance of a rolling ball than a ball that spends most of its time in the air.

Secondly, problems with accuracy increase as the club head rises during the backswing, i.e. swings vertically upward, because the higher the club head, the harder it is to return it correctly at impact. This is why it's not always a good idea to use your wedge on short shots or your putter on the long ones.

A properly executed putting stroke (with any club) keeps the club head low to the ground, and with this predominantly horizontal path in relation to the ground, you increase the chances of making dead center contact at impact. The advantage of contacting the ball on the sweet spot of your club face is that solid contact minimizes twisting of the club face, giving you an accurate roll.

While you can't always use your putter due to the length of the shot and/or the terrain, your next choice is to chip the ball using the club with the least loft so that it lands safely on the green. This allows your shot to hug the ground and take advantage of the accuracy of a rolling ball.

Rough in the *"chipping zone"*

If you play a course where there is thick rough in the "chipping zone", you may need to pitch the ball. The weight of your sand wedge helps to extract the ball from this difficult lie and you can still let the ball roll to the hole by using the "pitch and run technique."

The concept

The key concept for chipping is that a chip shot is merely a putt with a lofted club. The chip, as an extension of your putting stroke, is an offensive weapon that can keep your scores from soaring even though you're missing the greens. A chip shot played correctly provides an opportunity to hole out and, if you don't, you should leave yourself an easy putt.

The chip shot is used from five yards and in from the edge of the green. It's a low running shot with minimum flight time and maximum roll that lands about one yard onto the green and rolls to the hole like a putt.

In this chapter, you'll learn the flight-to-roll ratio that gives you the correct club for every situation, depending on the amount of flight and roll required for each shot. Regardless of the iron selected, by adapting it to function as much like your putter as possible, you can use the same pendulum motion for chipping that you do when putting.

For effective, accurate chipping, you should turn your iron into a putter.

The concept *continued*

Turning an iron into a putter

Top right: Like many good chippers, David Duval uses his putting grip in order to eliminate any wrist action.

Bottom right: When you raise a golf club on its toe, it aims to the right, so be sure it points at the target by squaring the face before you make your stroke.

There are three adjustments you should make that allow an iron to perform like your putter.

1 Raise your club on its toe to make the shaft upright like your putter. Just as in putting, this moves you closer to the ball with your eyes over the target line. However, raising any club on its toe aims the face to the right so to offset this, turn the club face in slightly until the top line of your club is perpendicular to the target line. This "toed in" position not only squares the club face to the target but also minimizes the destructive side spin that an open face imparts at impact.

When your club head is on its toe, use a pendulum motion for chipping to keep your club on the target line. Another advantage is that there is less surface on the bottom of your club head to catch in the grass so the club face remains square even if you hit a little behind the ball. If your club was fully soled, you'd pull your shot because the heel would dig in, twisting your club face to the left.

2 Grip down on your club until it matches the length of your putter. It is likely that you'll grip all the way down on your long irons and progressively less on the shorter irons to keep the length consistent with your putter. This not only allows you to bend until your eyes are over the line but also promotes maximum control. Your "chip grip" is actually your putter grip with your palms facing each other and the club handle positioned high in your palms to discourage wrist hinging.

3 Once you have turned your iron into a putter, use exactly the same type of stroke: a pendulum-style, shoulder-controlled motion, with minimal lower body movement and no wrist action.

The set up

The goal of your set up is to reduce side spin and excessive loft, both of which are the enemies of roll. The optimum chipping motion is one that creates over spin for a shot with minimum side spin and maximum roll. In this regard, one of the most important adjustments to reduce side spin and keep loft consistent is a grip that takes your wrists out of the stroke. The correct grip allows your arms to swing freely from the shoulder joints so your club moves down the target line with no opening or closing of the club face, and no addition of loft. Thus to be a good chipper, the loft you had at address is the loft you arrive with at impact.

Quiet
hands

Producing the right distance is much easier with quiet hands. Any time that wrist action is involved in the stroke, you add a speed producer and that affects your touch.

1

2

The hands stay quiet back and through the chipping motion (left). If your wrists flip (as shown below), you'll add loft to the club head and inaccuracy to your chip shots.

3

Finish like *you start*

Perhaps the most common fault in chipping is stopping the left arm just before impact. No matter how good your intentions are to have quiet hands as you chip, your hands become activated as soon as your arms stop. On the way back to the ball, your club head gathers momentum and, unless you keep your arms moving, the force in your club head pushes it past your hands, causing your left wrist to collapse. This changes the effective loft on the club face, so you could start a swing with 48 degrees and finish with 52 degrees, not a good technique if getting up and down is the game plan.

The set up *continued*

Stance width

In order to produce the necessary loft to carry the ball over the fringe you'll need to make some adjustments to your set up. Since the stroke motion requires no lower body action, your stance width is narrow. As in putting, not only is lower body movement unnecessary to the stroke motion but it is also detrimental. You won't have time for a weight transfer and you certainly don't need the power it provides.

Open stance

In chipping, you want to hit the ball with a descending blow, so place 80 percent of your weight on your left foot. Drop your left foot back from the target line and let your weight settle naturally into your left hip. This distribution anchors your lower body and encourages your weight to start, stay and finish on the left side.

Ball position

The ball is played opposite the inside of your right foot, with your hands positioned off the left thigh. With your weight on your left side, you easily produce the proper angle of attack, a naturally descending motion, without trying to "hit down" on the ball. With the ball so far back in your stance, your shoulders close, so draw your left foot back from the target line (opening your stance) until your shoulders arrive at the necessary square address position.

Distance from the ball

While the distance you stand from the ball depends on your body build, you should stand close enough so that your eyes are over the target line and your arms hang freely, straight down from your shoulders. The ball is played close to your feet, generally about six inches away. This puts the club's shaft in a vertical position that promotes a pendulum stroke. Set your hands well ahead of the ball, inclining your club shaft until it points to your left shoulder.

The stroke

Once you've set up correctly, your backswing is all shoulders and arms, without any hand or wrist action. Your shoulders control the stroke in both directions just as they do in the putting stroke. Throughout the chipping motion, your lower body stays quiet but not rigid. Actually, on longer chip shots you will need some turn so your arms can swing freely without bumping into your sides, but what movement there is should be reactive.

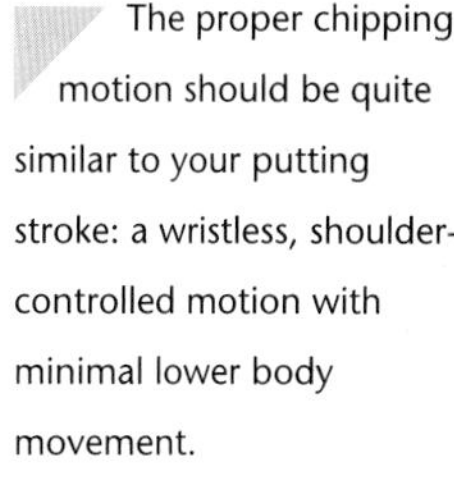

The proper chipping motion should be quite similar to your putting stroke: a wristless, shoulder-controlled motion with minimal lower body movement.

The stroke *continued*

Plan your chip as if it were a putt

Read the green and visualize your chip shot just as you would a putt. You should see in your mind's eye the target line, where you want the ball to begin its roll and the spot where you want the ball to finish. With the proper club selection and the appropriate adjustments all you need to think about is how hard you would hit a putt of the same distance. This may sound obvious but if you're faced with a curving chip, plan it like a putt. Set up on the line you want the ball to start on and stroke the chip down this line, allowing the slope of the green to take the ball to the hole.

How to pick a spot

Since it's not specifically prepared for roll, landing in the fringe of the green is unpredictable: bad bounces can destroy the line and soft turf can slow the ball down while hard spots can speed it up too much. Select a spot at least one yard on the green where you want your chip to land. This way you'll carry over the "trouble" and onto the safety of the green.

Choosing the right club

The most common chipping error occurs before you even set the club in motion: trying to manipulate the same club to fit all situations. Most golfers have a favorite club for chipping, like a pitching wedge or seven iron, one that feels the

most comfortable to them. However, be careful not to confuse comfort with correct. It is much easier to develop a good short game by using your full arsenal of irons, from a three iron through to a sand wedge, as the circumstances merit. This way, instead of adjusting your technique to your favorite club, you can fit the club to the shot, and the particulars of the situation.

To repeat, your goal should be to select the club with just enough loft to carry the ball one yard onto the green so that it rolls the rest of the way to the hole. This chipping style is employed by some of the best chippers in the world, such as Raymond Floyd, Nick Faldo and Tom Watson.

The key to consistent chipping can be summarized as follows: one stroke for all situations, with different clubs for different distances. The longer the chip shot, the less lofted (flatter faced) the club. The shorter the chip shot, the more lofted the club face.

The advantages

Our system has several advantages. In the first place, your putting stroke affords you the most touch, accuracy and distance control. Second, your putting stroke has the fewest moving parts and therefore the fewest variables and least margin for error. Third, you always have the club that will produce the correct flight-to-roll ratio. Fourth, your target is a landing area that is very close to you and is therefore easy to hit. Fifth, you'll use the same amount of energy (or stroke motion) for the chip shot as you would for a putt of equal distance, so when you practice chipping, you are also practicing putting and vice versa.

The flight-to-roll ratio

The club selection chart relates the ratio between the amounts of flight versus roll you get when chipping with each club.

Flight verus roll

Club	Flight	Roll
Sand wedge (11-iron)	1 part	1 part
Pitching wedge (10-iron)	1 part	2 parts
9-iron	1 part	3 parts
8-iron	1 part	4 parts
7-iron	1 part	5 parts
6-iron	1 part	6 parts
5-iron	1 part	7 parts
4-iron	1 part	8 parts
3-iron	1 part	9 parts

Here's how you should use this chart. Notice that the high-lofted clubs, such as your nine iron and wedge, have a much more even balance between flight time and roll time. Thus a chip with your sand wedge flies as far in the air as it rolls on the ground. Your higher-lofted clubs are used when the flag is cut close to the edge of the green with little room for roll.

As the area between the edge of the green and the cup increases in distance, you need more roll so your selection moves from the short irons, through the mid irons and finally to the long irons where the flight time is only one part and the roll time is nine parts. Since every chip shot requires some flight time to land on the green, don't use your one or two iron to chip with because they don't have enough loft.

The two constants

Keep in mind two constants for every chip: the landing area, which is always one yard on the green, and the number 12. The constant landing area, one yard on the green, gives you an easy target to hit and, in case you mis-hit the ball, enough margin for error to still have your ball land safely on the green.

Use the chart to understand the second constant, the number 12. Take, for example, a chip that requires one part flight and six parts roll. The chart tells you to select a six iron. Add the flight (six) to the club (six) and the sum is the constant 12. It's the same for all the clubs in the chart. Thus, the number 12 is the total of the club and roll added together.

Pitch or *chip?*

Even though your ball is in the chipping zone (inside five yards from the edge of the green) don't automatically assume you should chip the ball. The position of the hole relative to your target line may require you to pitch the ball. You may be two steps from the nearest part of the green but if you walk along your target line in the direction of the hole, the landing area may be nine steps from your ball. In this situation you'll need to pitch the ball to get the necessary loft and height to stop the ball quickly.

The advantages *continued*

The two variables

In addition to the two constants, there are two variables: the distance the ball flies in the air and the distance the ball rolls to the hole. To determine the club for the shot, calculate the ratio (or proportion) of flight to roll.

The flight-to-roll ratio

Once you've determined the line of your chip shot, you've automatically identified your first constant because your landing area is always on that line, one yard from the edge of the green. Now pace off the number of steps from your ball to the landing area. This determines your first variable: the amount the ball flies.

Keeping your stride width consistent, next pace off the distance from your landing area to the hole to determine your second variable: the amount the ball rolls. You now have enough information to calculate the flight-to-roll ratio using some simple arithmetic. All you do is create a fraction with your flight time on the top and your roll time on the bottom. Then reduce the fraction to 1 over the appropriate number. For example, the ratio of 5 steps of flight time over 15 steps of roll time, reduces to 1 over 3, one part flight and three parts roll.

The next step is to subtract the denominator (3) from the constant "12" to identify your chipping club, which in our example is a nine iron.

If the ratio isn't easily reducible, adjust the denominator to the nearest number that gives you a ratio that's easy to calculate in your head. Thus 3 over 13 would be adjusted to 3 over 12. You should also adjust the club depending on the slope of the green:

- Chipping uphill: add roll by choosing a five rather than a six iron.
- Chipping downhill: subtract roll by going from a six to a seven iron.

Keep in mind that the object of walking off the distance of your flight and roll is not to come up with an exact measurement. You are simply trying to find the proportion (or ratio) between the amount your ball needs to fly and the amount it needs to roll. Rarely will a situation present itself where, for example, your ball is precisely three yards from your landing area and then exactly nine yards to the hole. The proportion between the two is what's important, and that concept should guide you as you use your logic to adjust the numbers.

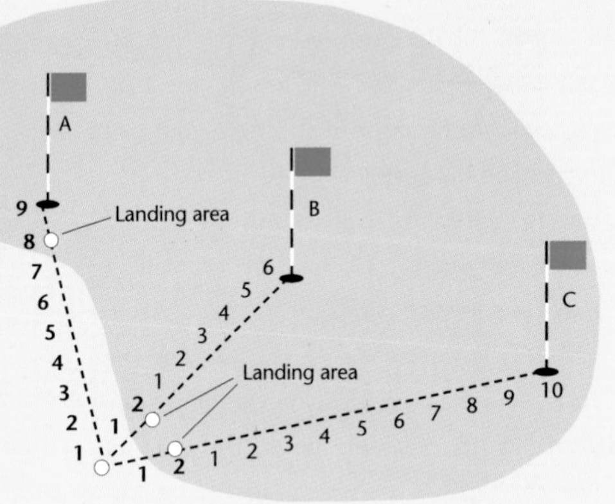

Flag A: although the ball is only a couple of yards off the green, you cannot chip to the flag because the landing area is 8 yards away, a pitch shot.
Flag B: 2 over 6 reduces to 1 over 3 (1 part flight and 3 parts roll); 3 from 12 is a nine iron.
Flag C: 2 over 10 reduces to 1 over 5 (1 part flight and 5 parts roll); 5 from 12 is a seven iron.

The three stages of learning

This method may seem complicated at first but with a little practice it becomes second nature. We've taught thousands of students, with excellent results, and you learn it in three stages.

- In the first stage, you actually walk off the distances and do the calculations.
- In the second stage, you've become so used to measuring the distances that your eyes take over and you no longer have to walk off the distances. You see every chip as one part flight and so many parts roll, and the ratio is automatic, based on your experience and practice.
- In the last stage, all the calculations as well as the club selection are done subconsciously, so you simply evaluate the shot and reach for the correct club.

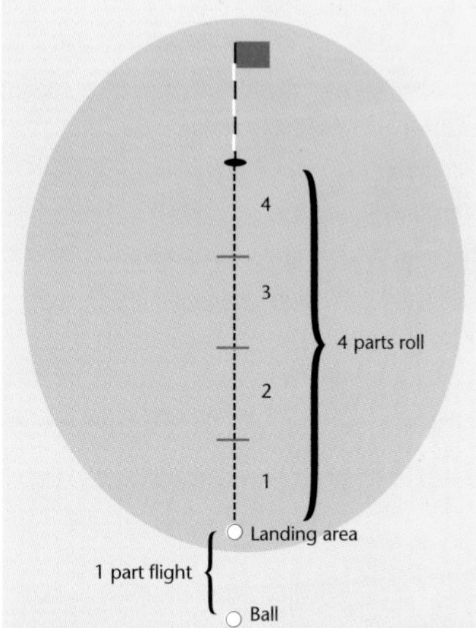

Eventually, you'll see every chip as one part flight with so many parts roll, and simply subtract the roll from 12 to get the correct iron.

Standardize *your stride*

Although your step doesn't have to be exactly one yard in length for our method to work (they must be consistent in length though), it's a good idea to match your stride to a yard, or a meter, since you'll be pacing off distances all over the course to determine your distance from the green. Use a tape measure and lay out ten yards. Then, using your normal stride, count how many steps you take within the ten-yard area. If you count twelve steps, for instance, a 20 percent error, adjust the length of your stride by making your steps longer until it matches the measurement of ten yards. That's your "golf stride" and it's usually longer than your normal stride.

Chipping drills

1 Path

Chip between two shafts to keep the path of your club head straight back and through. Lay two shafts parallel to each other to create a four-inch wide pathway to the green. Place a ball in the center of the path and practice hitting chips to the green. Make sure that the club head travels down this pathway in the straight back, straight through motion of the proper chipping stroke.

2 Wrist

Place a three iron under your left arm with the club head in the air and the grip end pointing toward the ground. Join the three iron grip to the grip of a five iron that you'll be chipping with, and hold both clubs with a putting grip. Chip a ball, and if your wrists are inactive the three iron shaft will finish away from your body. If you stop your arm swing through impact and use your wrists to hit the ball, the shaft of the three iron will hit your ribs, giving you feedback about your improper technique.

3 Weight

Using your right toe for balance only, hit chip shots with your right heel raised off the ground and the majority of your weight on your left side. Keeping your weight on your left side ensures that contact with the ball is made with a descending motion. If your wrists are too active, then check your finish position. If your weight is on your right side, you're forced to flip your wrists in order to get your club head "under the ball."

Chapter ten

Putting

The key to scoring in the game of golf is your play from inside 100 yards. This is where 64 percent of all golf shots are taken yet it is probably the most overlooked and under-practiced part of the game. The short game is often perceived as boring and not as "macho" or as exhilarating as giving the ball a hard whack with your driver. However, a good short game is the great equalizer, giving players of all abilities the opportunity to save strokes. By learning and utilizing a few fundamentals, and knowing which shots have the highest percentage of success in each situation, you can become a "scorer" as well as a player.

It is not an exaggeration to say that the majority of golfers prefer practicing with their driver instead of their putter even though, during the average round of golf, you employ your driver about 14 times while the putter is in your hands over 40 percent of the time. There is no question that the quickest way to lower your scores is to hole more putts.

Putting seems easy: the ball sits on what appears to be a finely manicured surface, with no obstacles, such as bunkers or water hazards, in the way. The hole is 4.25 inches wide while the ball is only about 1.68 inches around its circumference, so there's plenty of room for it in the cup. And the stroke itself is relatively short and simple, making physical strength a non factor. Thus the putting green is truly egalitarian, a place where players are separated only by their talent and their grit. However, whereas putting is an art that almost defies analysis, there are fundamentals that can make you a better putter.

The fundamentals of putting

By simply clapping your hands in front of you, you will learn three very important things about putting.

Although many styles have been successful, the modern pendulum motion keeps the putter face on line well past impact. Here Ernie Els demonstrates why he is a world-class player.

1 When you clap your hands they come together as a unit with your palms facing one another—it's the same when you grip the putter. Even though your hands are separated, your palms face each other so that your hands work as a unit—where the palm of your right hand faces so also does the back of your left hand. When your right palm points at the target, your putter faces down the target line.

2 When you clap your hands you also learn where the ball should be positioned in your stance. Since your hands meet naturally in the center of your body, all you have to do is grip your putter and bend from your hip joints until your putter head touches the ground. You'll find that in this position, the handle of your putter points to the center of your body. For the correct ball position, simply locate the ball just in front of your putter head and you will have identified the bottom of your swing arc.

3 And lastly, when you clap your hands you learn about the putting stroke itself. Note that in order to arrive together in the middle of your chest, each hand moves at an even, *pendulum-like* pace. This balance is what you want in your putting stroke so that your putter travels back and through without any attempt to increase or decrease its speed.

Putting technique

Once you are committed to the principles of the pendulum stroke, the first step to a consistent putting stroke is aiming your putter face correctly and properly aligning your shoulders and eyes to the target. How your club face is angled at impact determines the direction in which the ball deflects; where your shoulders point controls the direction in which your arms swing and therefore the path your club head follows; and it's your eye alignment that influences the path of your shoulders.

The set up

1 Set your putter directly behind the ball so that it is square to the target.

2 Next align your shoulders parallel left of the target line. A closed position at address (your shoulders pointing to the right of the target) causes your putter head to swing on an inside-to-out path that results in a putt pushed to the right. When your shoulders are open at address, your path is outside-to-in and the ball rolls to the left of target. Ideally, in the correct stroke, your putter moves along the target line as long as possible, both back and through the ball.

3 When you grip the putter, allow your hands to hang down comfortably so that they are directly below your shoulders. This puts your arms and hands in position for a straight back and through stroke. When your hands are positioned incorrectly, either outside or inside your shoulders, they try to get back under your shoulders as you swing, disrupting the path of your putter. When your hands are too close to your body, you will cut across the ball because your putter path is outside to in. When your hands are too far away from your body, your club head moves back inside the target line with the face open, closing on the through stroke. It is square for only an instant.

Eyes over *the ball*

Bend forwards until your eyes are directly over the ball. To locate the target, you need only rotate your head instead of disrupting your eye line by lifting your head. Since your visual system is a strong determiner of how your muscles move, your putting stroke follows your eye alignment—in essence, you putt where you look. How you position your eyes at address affects the alignment of your putter head.

- With your eyes outside your target line, you will see the hole as being left of where it really is and you'll miss a well-stroked putt to the left.
- With your eyes inside the target line, you'll mis-aim to the right, leaving a correctly putted ball to the right of the cup.

The putting stroke

There are two motions in golf: a swing motion and a stroke motion.

- The swing motion is lower body oriented with plenty of wrist action, both of which combine to produce power. This motion is used for long shots.
- The stroke motion is upper body oriented and does not use any wrist action. This motion is used in putting and chipping where accuracy is at a premium and only minimal force is needed. Therefore, in the stroke motion you grip the club in a way that quietens your hands.

Set your hands on the club with your palms facing each other, square to the target line. Place the grip of the putter in the life line of your left hand to eliminate wrist action. The back of your left hand and the palm of your right hand face the target with your thumbs on top of the handle. You gain feel from your thumb and index finger so, by putting your thumbs on top of the shaft, you put your "feelers" in position to work for you.

1

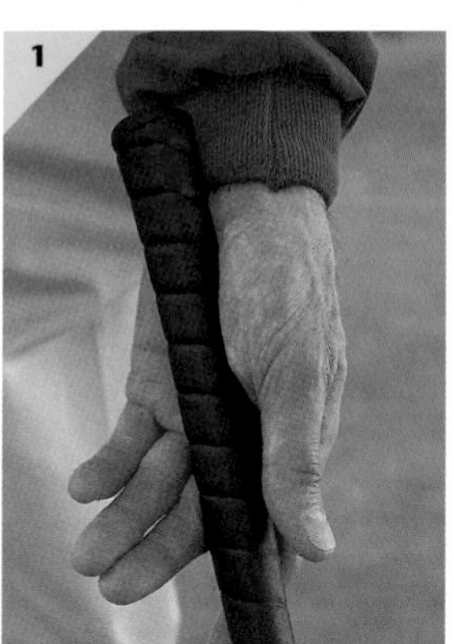

2

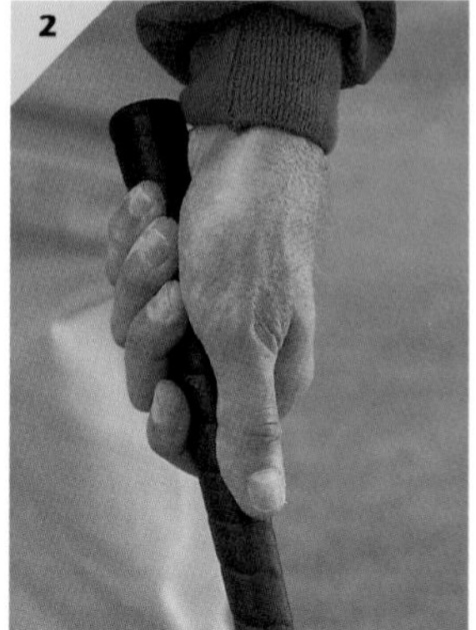

3

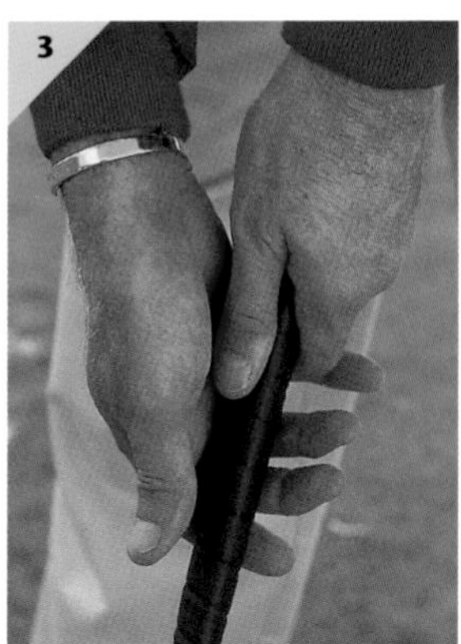

4

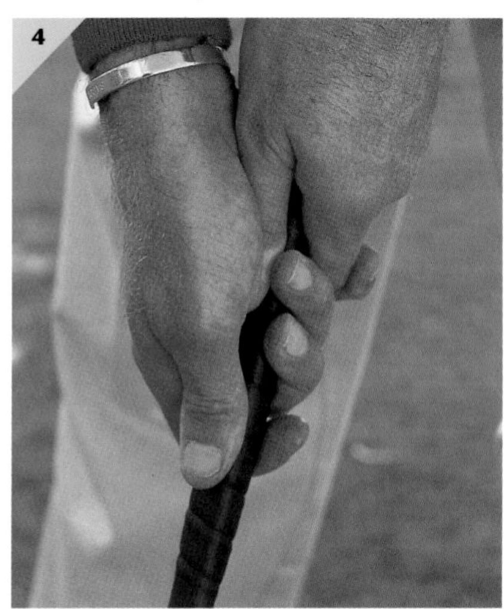

5

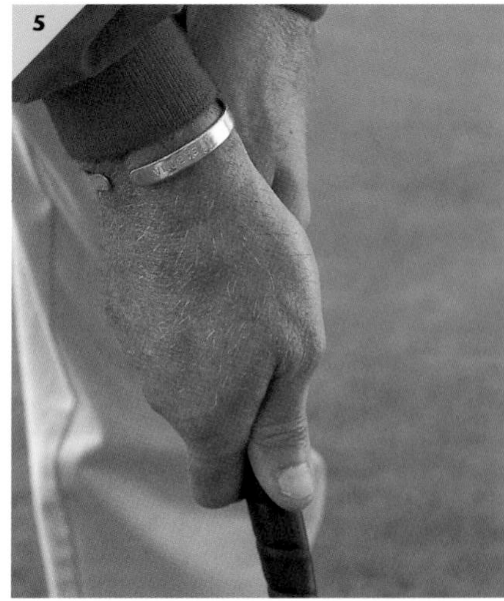

The stroke motion

While your hands move as a unit you can understand how each one coordinates with the other as follows: to feel the correct motion of your left hand take your normal putting stance, then place your right hand on your left shoulder. With no backswing, simply push the ball toward the hole using only your left hand to operate the putter. This drill will help you understand the relationship between the back of your left hand and the putter face because you must keep the back of your left hand facing your target throughout the stroke for the ball to roll accurately.

After hitting a few of these "push putts", add your right hand to the club but keep your fingers open and extending down the shaft so that your palm faces the target. Use your right palm to push the ball toward the target, focusing on how your right palm exerts energy through the face of your putter in the direction of the target. As in other sports (for example, dribbling a basketball), the direction in which you exert energy is always the direction your palm is facing.

Note: there's a key angle created when you place your right hand on the putter. Your right wrist bends backward slightly toward your forearm. Many successful putters keep this angle intact through impact to prevent over-use of their hands.

The stroke itself

Your stroke utilizes the top of your spine as the anchor point around which your shoulders rock. This point remains stationary as the triangle formed by your shoulders and arms moves like a see-saw. The triangle must maintain its shape throughout the stroke with the distance between the elbows constant, ensuring that the bottom of the putting arc also remains constant.

The stroke itself is very similar to the swinging motion of the pendulum in a grandfather clock. This stroke works well on all types of putting surfaces and is most effective with a center-shafted putter.

Greg Norman's shoulders have rotated around the top of his spine, which is the basic fundamental of the modern putting motion.

Your *forearms*

In addition to quiet hands, you should arrange your forearms so they operate as a unit. Your left forearm should be directly in front of the putter shaft and your right forearm directly behind it. Your forearms are level with neither forearm higher nor lower than the other.

Your *knees*

Bend your knees until your weight is on your heels, pinching your knees toward each other to eliminate any lower body movement during your putting stroke. One of the differences between a stroke and a swing is that in the stroke, there's no lower body action.

Your *feet*

Position your feet equidistant from the target line and parallel left to that line. Your stance width varies according to comfort and your body build but at least 60 percent of your weight should be solidly on your left side and it should stay there as you putt.

The putting stroke *continued*

The *pendulum stroke*

The principles of the pendulum stroke as follows—acceleration without effort, force without manipulation. Never add or subtract any energy from your putting stroke. As in the full swing, you'll do your best putting when there is more of physics and less of you involved in the stroke—more let and less make.

The pendulum stroke

A lot has been said about accelerating the putter head through impact. While it is true that your club head is moving faster at the lowest point of its arc due to gravity, when you try to add speed to your putter, the heel beats the toe to the ball, leaving the club face open. The opposite happens when you force yourself to make a long and stylish back stroke. The odds are that you will over-do it and swing back too long, forcing you to slow down your putter as it approaches the ball, which tends to shut the club face, allowing the toe of your putter head to pass the heel.

1

The best way to putt is to forget about trying to manipulate the putter and simply let the principles of the pendulum putting stroke work for you. With the correct pendulum motion there is no conscious "hit" yet your club face is accelerating at impact with the face square to the target line. If you let the image of the pendulum be in control, where the arc on one side of the low point is equal to the arc on the other, your putting stroke naturally finds the correct length and force.

2

3

4

The basics of putting

1 Hold your club in the life line of your left hand with your palms facing each other, square to the target.
2 Aim your club face square to the target, and sole your putter head directly behind the golf ball.
3 Align both eyes down the target line. Position your dominant eye over the ball.
4 Align your shoulders parallel to the target line.
5 Position your hands directly beneath your shoulders.
6 Set your feet parallel left to the target line, pinching both knees toward each other with your weight on your heels.
7 Maintain your forearms on the same plane parallel to each other.
8 Point the butt of your club at the middle of your spine.
9 During your takeaway, allow your left shoulder to work under as your right shoulder works up so that your shoulders control the stroke like a see-saw.
10 Maintain a constant distance between your elbows while you putt.
11 Keep your head still while you putt.
12 Maintain the angle of your right wrist throughout the stroke.

See-saw *drill*

The drill below develops the see-saw motion of your shoulders. Place a club shaft under both arms just above your elbows. If your stroke is correct, the shaft works up and down like a see-saw, parallel to the target line. If your stroke is incorrect, the shaft works around your shoulders and points well left of target upon completion of the stroke.

Putting strategy

Preparation plays an important role in the success or failure of every putt. On the greens, you must first study (read) your putt to determine the amount of break, the slope and how much speed you'll need.

Reading the greens

Always make your initial read from behind the hole looking back down the target line to your ball. From here you will see the general direction of the break. Give special attention to the area around the hole because the effect of the break is more pronounced as your ball slows down. Also check your line for ball marks, pebbles and anything else that might knock your ball off line.

Once you have established the dominant break, move to the low side of the putt to determine the amount of slope and its inclination. When you stand on top of a mountain and look down at the valley, it looks flat but when you stand at the base of the mountain and look up, you can see the slope and inclination. Take care to stand equidistant from the ball, target line and the cup in order to maintain your perspective. This triangulation gives you a much truer reading.

Your final read is from behind the ball. Here, determine your line and select the spot (as in bowling) to roll your ball over. Also, in lining up behind the ball, stand on the line on which you want your ball to start. For straight putts, this is the target line, but to give you the proper perspective for a putt that curves, stand on the curved line or arc of the putt—not on the target line.

Drainage *patterns*

When your ball rolls across a putting surface the major influence on its direction is the slope of the green. Sometimes any contours are difficult to see but an understanding of how an architect designs a putting green helps you to evaluate the effect of slope more accurately. A well-designed putting surface has drainage patterns that draw water off to the sides away from the center of the green. In general, you can expect swales to channel the water away from the bunkers and toward the ponds and lakes. Changes in grass color surrounding the green and damage from past accumulations of water are also clues to how the drainage flows.

Putting strategy *continued*

Reading the greens

Good putting also requires reading the grain. The direction in which the grass grows, or what is commonly referred to as grain, affects the distance and direction of your putt.

When you are practicing, you can test the grain by lightly dragging your putter across the grass. If the grass stands up, you've scraped your putter against the grain; if it stays down, you are with the grain. When you're playing, the rules of golf don't permit you to test the green in this manner, but you can test the collar or apron of the green without penalty. Just make sure it's the same kind of grass as the putting surface before you include the information in your reading.

Grain affects both the curve and speed of your putt. Putting directly against the grain slows your putt down; putting with the grain adds speed. If the grain runs across the line of your putt in the same direction as the slope of the green, it increases the break as the ball slows down. Note that side-grain slows down your putt almost as much as putting straight into the grain.

Tropical climate grasses, such as Bermuda, grow westward toward the setting sun. The characteristically thick, coarse Bermuda grows in an upward swirl and its grain is strong and influential on the speed and direction of your putts. The finer-leafed grasses, such as Bent, lie down and grain is not a major factor. This type of grass is common in cooler climates and what little grain it has often grows toward the natural water supply.

When the sun shines on a green you can judge the direction of the grain by the appearance of the grass. If the grass looks dark and dull, the grain is growing toward you. If the grass looks shiny, the grain is growing away from you.

Which type of putt?

Now that you have read the green, you are ready to decide which type of putt is called for. There are three ways to make a putt.

- You can "die" the ball into the cup, so that its last roll barely carries it over the edge as it falls into the cup.
- You can "send" the ball into the cup at the optimum speed. Here, the ball contacts the backside of the metal cup about halfway down.
- You can "firm" the ball into the cup, where every putt is played as a straight one and the ball strikes the dirt on the back of the hole, just above the metal cup.

One advantage of the "dying" putt is that there are "three entrances" that your slowly moving ball can use to fall into the cup: the front of the cup and the two sides. Another advantage is that if you miss, your ball always finishes next to the hole. However, there are also some disadvantages. With a slight miscalculation, the dying putt won't get to the cup. And, because of its slow speed, the break is increased and the ball is easily knocked off line by the imperfections in the green. The "dying" putt is best utilized for long putts, putts with a lot of break, downhill putts and/or when the greens are so fast you must "cozy" your putt up to the hole.

The advantages of the "firm" putt are that it eliminates the break and, because of its speed, it holds its line despite imperfections on the green. The disadvantages are that the size of the hole is effectively reduced because the ball is moving too fast to sneak in the sides of the cup and, if it misses the hole, you'll have some work left on your next putt. This type of putt is most effective on short uphill putts.

The "optimum speed" putt does not have any disadvantages. The hole is its true size, the break and imperfections are minimized, the ball always gets there and, if it rolls by the hole, you get information about your next putt by watching the break. If you miss the optimum speed putt, the ball only travels a short distance past the hole.

The optimum speed as calculated by Dave Peltz, the American putting expert, carries your ball about 17 inches past the hole. Remember that the tour professionals who offer the advice to "die" the ball in the hole, play on perfect greens but for most amateurs, the greens are bumpy, the cups are crowned and located on slopes. If you hit a "dying" putt under these conditions it can be knocked off line or mis-directed by the crown of the cup.

Short putting

On short putts, the "never up-never in" theory applies. You should keep this philosophy in mind on any putt that you feel you can make, and it should be a normal, built-in part of your putting strategy. Being aggressive on these putts not only assures that your ball will reach the target but also makes it less susceptible to the effects of spike marks and foot prints around the cup.

When you can see into the hole from your address position, pick a spot on the back of the cup liner and putt to it. This increases your accuracy by forcing you to focus on a smaller target, one you can miss and still make the putt.

1

2

3

4

5

Lagging

Lagging a very long putt into one-putt range is a special skill. Conventional wisdom advises golfers to aim their approach putts into a three-foot circle around the cup, but when the pin is on a slope, as is often the case, not all "three footers" are equal. If you have played any golf at all, you know that three footers from above the hole or from a side slope can be score wreckers.

With this in mind, try to make it, but if it does not go in, your approach should be directly below the hole so you can confidently stroke your next putt straight back up the hill into the cup. When your task is to lag your ball down in two, where you putt from on your second putt is as important as how well you stroke it.

Be *realistic*

Avoid making unnecessary changes in your putting stroke just because you miss some putts. A high percentage of your misses are due to imperfections on the putting surface, such as footprints, spike marks, etc. Research shows that over the course of a year, the average tour professional misses 53 percent of putts from six feet. This tells you two things:

1 Keep your expectations realistic in order to preserve both your putting stroke and your self image.

2 Get the ball closer than six feet with your chips, pitches and lag putts.

1

2

3

4

5

6

Most good lag putters don't use the "three-foot circle" theory, and we don't recommend it. Good putters try to hit the ball into the hole, not three feet from it. From a long distance it is easy to leave your putt three feet short of where you want it to stop and, if you miss the three-foot circle by that much, you are six feet from the hole.

For long putts, have a friend attend the flag stick so that you're not searching for the hole when you take your last look at the target. You'll have better depth perception if he stands behind the hole.

Tip: a tip that will help your lag putting is to strike the ball solidly by concentrating on a dimple on the back of the ball so that your head stays *still* until your ball is well under way. Off-center hits leave you that "nettlesome" six-foot distance, so after you've figured out the distance and the break, focus on solid contact.

Making *solid contact*

Find the sweet spot on your putter and mark it, because good putting requires solid contact and this comes from hitting the sweet spot. Note that a putter's sweet spot is not necessarily in the exact center of the blade. You can find it as follows: using only your thumb and index finger, suspend your putter so that it hangs vertically. Tap the face of the putter with a golf ball so that it swings back and forth. When the blade goes straight back with no side-to-side movement or twisting, that's your sweet spot. Then mark it with some paint.

Pre-shot routine

When you have chosen your line and decided on the type of putt you're going to hit, take a practice stroke next to your ball, looking at the hole, to program your mind for the distance of the putt. By doing this your eyes register the distance to the target and your brain calculates how much energy is required. For an uphill putt, take your practice stroke further from the hole than your ball lies to account for the added force you'll need because of the slope. If it is a downhill putt, stand closer to the hole to program hitting the putt easier.

Next, take another practice stroke, this time looking at the ball, and then slide your putter forward so that the sweet spot is directly behind the ball.

Set your feet in position and look down the line to the hole counting one; bring your eyes back to the ball on two; draw the putter back on three; and through to the ball on the count of four. Your goal, using the count of one, two, three, four, is to eliminate any need to think about putting mechanics. Once you ingrain this routine, your stroke will be automatic.

1

2

3

Putting drills

The purpose of doing drills is to repeat the feeling of the skill you're trying to learn and, once the new motion is perfect, to over-ride old habits through repetition and reinforcement. Here are some drills that will help you to perfect your putting stroke once you know what you should be doing when you stroke a putt.

Look at the hole drill

Take your stance and simply stroke your putt while looking at the hole instead of your ball. This will help you to stay focused on your target instead of thinking too much about the mechanics of your stroke.

Three shaft drill

Place three shafts on the green at ten-foot intervals from your ball. Putt your first ball to the shaft furthest from you, approximately 30 feet away. Putt the second ball to the middle shaft, 20 feet away. Putt the third ball to the shaft closest to you, about 10 feet away. When playing, you're always faced with different distance putts and this drill helps you to adapt quickly.

Ladder drill with tee

Mark your starting position with a tee 12 inches from the hole and hit three putts. If you hole all three, move away from the hole another six inches so you're 18 inches from the hole. As long as you make three out of three putts at each tee, progress in increments of six inches farther from the hole. If you make fewer than three out of three, return to the previous tee. Having to make all three putts before you advance simulates the pressure of putting out on the course.

Square club face drill

Find a flat area on the putting green about 10 feet from the cup. Position a ball with a stripe around its equator so the stripe points directly down the target line. Stroke the ball to the hole and observe the rotation. If your putter face is square to the target line and you've made a good stroke the stripe will revolve end over end with very little wobble.

Ladder drill

The object of this drill is to develop your feel for distance. Place five balls on the putting green. Putt the first ball five feet and, without looking up, putt the second ball 10 feet. Continue with the remaining balls, spacing them five feet apart. Doing this drill helps you to feel the amount of shoulder motion you need to create each distance.

Pendulum driver drill

Place the grip end of your driver against your stomach about four inches below your sternum. Slide your hands down the shaft to match the length of your putter and align your forearms with the grip end of the shaft. Bend from the hips until your driver soles on the ground. Make your putting stroke keeping the butt of the grip in your stomach and feel your arms and shoulders stroke the ball without any flipping of your wrist. This drill is great for eliminating wrist action.

Ball curve
drill

This drill teaches you how to control distance and direction and how to read breaks. Choose a putt about 15 feet long which has a noticeable break. Putt one ball to get the line of your putt. Then position seven balls along the line of the putt, each two feet apart. Putt the closest ball into the hole and work backward, putting each ball over the spot where the previous ball lay.

Sweet spot
drill

Rub some chalk on your putter face so that when you stroke a putt, the ball leaves a powdery mark, indicating where you made contact. Start with some short putts, and when you make perfect contact five times in a row, extend your distance by 10 feet.

Chapter eleven

Bunker play

John Daly's strength and length are negated by the lie of his ball in this fairway bunker. The best he can do in this circumstance is to wedge it out to the safety of the fairway.

Most people call them "traps" revealing how they feel about hitting into the sand, but you won't find the word trap in the rules of golf—the hazards filled with sand are termed bunkers and good bunker play starts not only with the right club but also with the right attitude. Having the right attitude, a positive and confident one, comes from knowing the proper technique which makes bunker play relatively simple. Remember that rule number one in the bunker is always to get out on your first attempt.

The correct club is a sand wedge, specially designed to make bunker play easy. It was invented by Gene Sarazen, who soldered lead on the bottom of his pitching wedge, or what was then known as a "niblick," so its leading edge wouldn't dig into the sand. So effective was his invention that he kept a towel over his bag to prevent his opponents from copying his secret weapon. They soon caught on, however, and Wilson Sporting Goods made popular what is now a staple in every golfer's bag—the sand wedge.

Green side bunker shots

There are two types of green side bunker shots depending on the lie of the ball.

- The first situation is a good lie where your ball sits nicely on top of the sand.
- The second lie is not good because your ball is buried in the sand.

Each type of lie requires a different technique: when your lie is good, you'll use the splash shot; and when your ball is buried, you'll hit an explosion or blast shot. One clue to the technique is in the image words used to describe the shot—"splash" for the good lie, "blast" for the bad.

Splash shot particulars

When your ball sits on top of the sand you'll use the splash shot, where your goal is to contact the sand before you hit the ball. One way to think about it is that the sand shot is one of the few shots in golf you try to hit fat. All that is required is the displacement of sand at the back of and beneath the ball, which lifts your ball into the air so it rides to the green on a cushion of sand.

Unfortunately, some golfers attempt to pick the ball off the sand, clearly a dangerous technique

The sand wedge: designed to work in the bunker

As described in our equipment section, your sand wedge is a high-lofted club with a flange underneath its face to displace sand, thereby enabling your club head to slide through the sand rather than digging down into it. The idea is to take a thin strip of sand with measurements similar to those of a dollar bill, rather than the "bucket" of sand that most golfers think they need.

The unique feature that allows you to shave the sand is called bounce. Look at the sole of your sand wedge and you'll notice that it is lower than the leading edge. Bounce is a correction factor which allows your club to skim through the sand rather than dig. As you'll see, maximizing bounce is essential to the proper execution of the splash shot, whereas reducing bounce is the key to the proper execution of the explosion shot.

- Flange is a term used to describe the area of the sole from the leading edge to the back of the club.
- Bounce defines the angle from the leading edge to the back of the club.

1

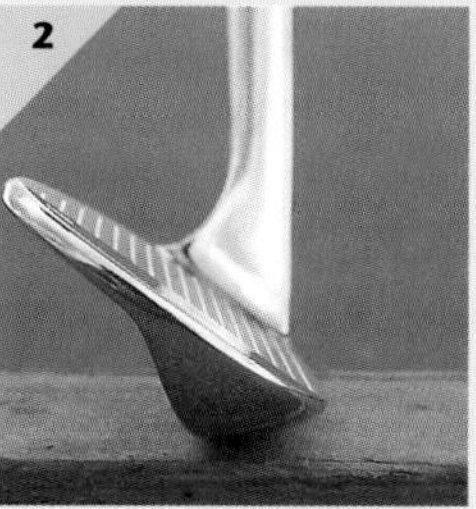

2

Mechanics of *the splash shot*

1 Position the ball forward in your stance.

2 Open your club face and then take your grip.

3 Open your stance until your club face aims to the target, keeping the butt of the club at the center line of your body.

4 Stand further from the ball and dig your feet into the sand to lower the bottom of your swing arc.

5 Make sure that your head is directly between your shoulders, not tilted.

6 Swing down your shoulder line and keep your weight on your left side throughout your swing.

Green side bunker shots *continued*

that often leads to thin, bladed shots that travel much too far. Other golfers have the idea that the ball must be "blasted" out of the bunker so they take too much sand, producing shots that travel too short a distance and often don't get out of the bunker.

With skulled shots that fly over the green and muffed shots that stay in the bunker, it's no wonder that the average golfer approaches the bunker shot with trepidation—yet, as we shall see, once your technique is correct, the sand shot loses much of its intimidation.

Fundamentals of the splash shot

For the splash shot, always open your club face to maximize the bounce. The shorter the shot, the more open your club face. And be sure to always open the club face before you finalize your grip on the club. Do this by hovering your club head above the ball using only your right hand to aim the club face to the right of the target. Then take your grip with both hands, keeping your club face in place. The problem with taking your grip first, then rolling your arms to open the club face to the ball, is that doing it this way, your arms roll over through impact, returning the club face to square or, worse, closing the club face.

Secondly, with the butt end of your club pointing at the center line of your body, open your stance by pulling your left foot away from the target line until your club face aims to the target. By opening your stance, you effectively shorten the length of your left leg and plant your weight in your left hip. This provides a stable platform that encourages you to hit down and through the shot. To execute the splash shot properly your club swings along your shoulder line, so you should position the ball forward in your stance off your left heel. This opens your shoulders, producing an outside to in swing path that carves the ball out of the sand.

In taking your stance, work your feet into the sand for stability. With your feet below the ball it guarantees that you'll hit behind the ball, a necessary feature of the splash shot. It also allows you to test the consistency and texture of the sand—information that you need in order to calculate where to contact the sand and how hard to hit the shot. However, take note that when you dig your feet in, you effectively move the hosel of the club closer to the ball, so adjust by standing farther from the ball. For every inch you lower yourself into the sand, move back an inch from the ball.

The final set up key involves the position of your head and spine. It's vital that you hold your head in the center of your body with no spinal tilt toward the left or, the more common error, toward your right shoulder. The weight of your head is significant so if your head and spine lean toward your right shoulder, the rest of your body weight does also, tilting your entire body out of position.

The swing itself is upper-body oriented because your weight starts, stays and finishes on your left side. Your arms swing fully allowing the club to move along your shoulder line.

The Quadrant *method*

In your practice draw two perpendicular lines in the sand and number the quadrants clockwise from one to four. One line points to your target, the other to the ball of your left foot. Place your golf ball where the two lines meet This ensures that the ball is positioned well forward in your stance and encourages you to hit the sand first. Open your stance and be sure to swing your club head into quadrant three on the backswing, then along your shoulder line into quadrant one on your through swing. Note that your club at no time enters quadrant four as it would if you were set square to the target line.

Your three-to-one swing path promotes a cut-across swing action that allows the bounce of your sand wedge to slice through the sand to give you the soft-landing splash shot you need.

With your weight fixed on your left side, the swing is dominated by your upper body, primarily your arms and shoulders. Notice that while there is minimal lower body action (hips and knees are very quiet) during the backswing, the downswing exhibits an active lower body that allows the club head to slide under the ball using the bounce rather than the leading edge.

The short *splash shot*

Occasionally you'll be faced with a very short bunker shot, one you need to land softly next to a pin tucked near the bunker. You'll play this shot in much the same way as a regular splash shot using your low-gear swing speed, except that you'll open your stance until you're almost facing the target. But with such an open BASE be sure that your ball is positioned off your left heel, because unless you adjust, the open stance moves the ball back in your stance—too far to the rear for the high shot you need.

In addition to your stance, open the face of your club until it points well right of your target. By opening the face, the loft of your club is increased, causing the ball to fly higher and shorter.

One mistake that's often made in this situation is to forward press the hands until they're ahead of the ball. This takes loft off your shot and moves the hosel dangerously closer to the ball, so take care to keep the butt of the club at the center line of your body to create the high shot you need.

Green side bunker shots *continued*

Face, base and pace: controlling the distance

You can become a bunker ace by utilizing an easy to remember system called "face, base and pace" that will help you to set up correctly and to control the distance of your splash shots.

- The first part of the system, FACE, refers to the club face, which is the first distance control determinant. The more you open the club face, the higher and shorter the ball travels. So first determine the amount of loft necessary to clear the lip of the bunker and then assess the total distance required for the shot, opening the club face the appropriate amount.
- The second part of our system refers to your BASE. Open your stance (your BASE) to a point where your club face readjusts from its open position to aim directly at your target. Next determine how far you want to hit behind the ball. You learn this by practicing but, in general, the farther you hit behind the ball the shorter your shot; the less sand you take, the longer the shot.
- The third control feature of our system is the PACE of your swing. The shorter the shot the slower your pace; the longer the shot the faster your pace. You limit the length of your swing by opening your BASE and alter the distance by adjusting the FACE and PACE.

Once you know the FACE and the BASE, controlling the distance that your shot travels is much like the windshield wiper system that maintains three separate speeds, each with a constant speed back and through.

- For the long bunker shot your entire swing is on high.
- For the medium distance it's on medium speed.
- For the short distance it's low speed.

The board drill

Bury a painted 2 x 4 inch board, about16 inches long, in the sand so that the four-inch side of the board is level with the sand. Without a ball, address the middle of the board and swing your club as described above, allowing the bounce of your club head to hit the board. Check your club head—if the leading edge has paint on it your swing was incorrect; if the bounce has paint on it, you're using the flange as you should.

Now place a pile of sand on top of the board and, using the same motion, let the bounce hit the board causing the sand to fly onto the green. Next, place a ball on top of a pile of sand and once again simply allow the bounce of your club head

to hit the board. Both the ball and the sand will fly onto the green.

You'll feel the correct motion of the splash shot because the board will force you to swing correctly. Once you get the feeling of your club head bouncing rather than digging, place a ball on the sand next to the board and reproduce the "splash" feeling while hitting a sand shot from a normal lie. If you have trouble, go back to the board until you can hit the splash shot correctly every time.

The buried bunker shot

Playing from a buried lie is quite different from playing a ball that's sitting nicely on top of the sand. Since your ball is below the surface, you want your club to make a deep cut into the sand to dig the ball out. To accomplish this, position your ball halfway between the middle of your stance and your right foot, then close your club face to square it back to your target. With the leading edge exposed and the bounce eliminated, your club plows into the sand and, by using a combination of hands and arms, you can swing abruptly up and down, creating a descending blow behind the ball. This descending blow, along with the closed club face, allows your club to dig deeply into the sand causing the ball to pop out.

Unlike the splash shot, don't try for a follow through; if you do it correctly you'll leave your club head in or very near the sand at the completion of your swing. With a shot like this you produce minimal back spin so your ball comes out low and running. Too often, golfers try to lift the ball out of a buried lie and end up hardly advancing it at all. Proper technique eliminates this problem. However, be careful; even the pros have trouble controlling this shot, so know your limitations and just get the ball on the green.

Mechanics of *the blast shot*

1 Position the ball back in your stance.

2 Close the club face until it is square to the target.

3 Using a combination of arms and hands, strike a descending blow just behind the ball, without trying to follow through.

4 Allow for very little back spin, a lower trajectory and more roll.

1 Drop your left foot back to level your hips and set your weight into the slope.

2 Because of the necessary steep angle of attack, your club head makes a deep cut into the sand and causes limited follow through.

Determining
the loft

If you're unsure how to determine the loft an iron produces try this technique. Pick a club that you think may be right. Lay it down in the grass, adjacent to your position in the bunker, with the butt end of the club pointing in the direction you want your ball to fly. Step on the club face and the butt end rises up. This angle is an indication of the approximate amount of loft you can expect from that iron. Remember that you can't let your club touch the sand so don't try this in the bunker unless you're just practicing.

Fairway bunker shots

Fairway bunker shots rate among the most difficult in the game for the average player. This is because most people don't know how to plan these shots or how to execute them.

The "three Ls" of club selection

In assessing a fairway bunker shot your first consideration is the conditions of play. Before making your club selection, be sure to check the "three Ls":

- The *lie* of the golf ball.
- The *lip* of the bunker.
- The *length* of the shot.

The lie of the ball determines the type of shot that you can play. The lip determines which club you'll need to produce the necessary trajectory to clear it. And your last consideration is the length of the shot.

- If your ball sits beneath the level of the sand, regardless of the length you want to hit the ball, you may have to take a sand wedge and dig it out.
- If you have a good lie, where the ball is resting on top of the sand and can be hit cleanly, check the lip of the bunker. You'll need a club that gives you sufficient loft to safely clear the lip of the bunker. Since proper fairway bunker technique shortens the standard distance you hit an iron, you'll need to hit one more club, so include that in your calculation of sufficient loft if the lip allows.

You can only consider the length of the shot if the lie and the lip conditions allow it. If you need to hit a four iron to get to the green but the lip requires the trajectory of a seven iron, you'll have to go with the seven. When the lie and lip are favorable, only then can you consider the length of the shot.

The set up

The last outcome you want is to leave your ball in the bunker so, unless you're an expert, the guideline is never to use more than a four iron in a fairway bunker. With the long irons and fairway woods it's hard enough to get the ball airborne from a good lie in the fairway, so leave them in the bag when you have to contend with the sand and the lip of a bunker.

Begin your address proceedings by choking down on the handle of your club about an inch. This allows you to make a more controlled swing. Play the ball in the middle of your stance to help you pick it cleanly off the sand. Stand a little farther from the ball than you normally do and reach for it by stretching your arms away from your body—this helps prevent hitting the sand behind the ball, the most common mistake in a fairway bunker.

It also helps to widen and open your stance, anchoring your left foot with 60 percent of your weight, and wedging your right foot into the sand with your right knee angled in toward the target. Your shoulders should be square, even though your feet and hips are open.

The swing itself: think "pick"

The controlling concept for the fairway bunker shot is to pick the ball off the sand, so if you make a mistake it's much better to hit the ball thin than fat. Some golfers even try to catch it a little thin to protect against hitting the sand first. Once you have the concept (think pick), keep your lower body relatively quiet during the shot. The swing should be a three-quarter motion with most of your weight remaining in your left hip throughout your swing. By reducing weight transfer, you decrease the risk that you'll sink into the sand at the top of your swing—a sure way to hit sand before you contact the ball.

Chapter twelve

The inner game

Fuzzy Zoeller's care-free style and "whistle while you work" attitude is the envy of any golfer who has ever struggled with his composure on the golf course.

What separates the three levels of golfers: those that can't play a lick, those who can play when it doesn't really count, and those who can play no matter what's at stake? Well, as you can imagine, this is a complicated question with an even more complicated set of answers but one difference is this: the poor player is hardly ever committed to the shot; the good player is committed to the shot before he hits it; but the great player is committed to the shot while he is swinging!

Most golfers aren't committed because they never get the shot they need to play clear in their mind. They're worried about *not* doing something—"Don't hit it left; don't hit it in the water." Playing by "don'ts" won't get it done because no commitment is possible and with the fuzzy set of instructions to "don't do something," your brain is a poor commander in directing your army of muscles to swing the club correctly.

Playing by "do's" won't do either

Some golfers play by "do's", usually the mid-level player who has a brain full of information—"keep the right arm tucked; stay down; take it away low and slow." This is the DO-DO system and it puts your brain on alert that it needs to get consciously involved in a complicated motor activity (your downswing) that takes less than 0.05 seconds. This is not a good plan because if you're still calculating what to do while you're doing it, your chances for a good swing are drastically reduced.

Get committed to play your best golf

Great players decide on the shot they want to play and then stay with that decision while they swing. One way to keep your commitment from start to finish is to use images that are so compelling that they rivet your attention on your plan. If your image of the shot is strong and clear, all your resources are dedicated to making it a reality.

The power of imagery

Your mental images are created as you process information about your world and these images then cue your motor responses. When you're late, you run after a taxi; when you're scared you run away from the tiger. How your muscles get the job done—the technique of running—is done by unconscious competence; you don't have to think about it as you do it. If you did, the chances are you'd be late—or would get eaten!

But when you swing a golf club the urge to think about it while you do it is very strong. This puts your conscious mind in control and in the less than half a second it takes for your swing back to the ball, you don't have much time for conscious instructions. You're "in your own way". That's why Ben Hogan said that "the downswing is no place to give yourself a lesson".

An example of getting out of your own way is Terry Larson, who played a round of "speed golf" on the run in just under 40 minutes, shooting 75. The day before in his practice round he spent three-and-a-half hours playing the course and shot 77. He offered this explanation: "When you play sports like baseball or tennis you react to the target. In golf the ball just sits and you can end up thinking too much. In speed golf you run up to the ball, find the target and hit it."

Now if you haven't learned to swing your club correctly then reread the appropriate sections of this book or see your teaching professional, because imagining your ball tight to the hole won't help much if you don't know how to hit a seven iron. However, once you learn the basics of how to swing the club, to play your best golf you need to step aside and let imagery take control.

So if you're not thinking about swing mechanics while you swing, what are you supposed to think about? The answer is to occupy your mind with images by using your imagination.

Dr. Rod Borrie uses flotation tanks to help his patients' image. He says: "The conscious brain can process only about seven bits of information at one time, but complex movements such as athletic movements are made up of far more than seven bits of information." Thus to play your best golf, turn the complicated movements of your golf swing over to your unconscious competence.

Playing by images serves two purposes:

1 Images occupy your mind while you are swinging, leaving no room for the paralyzing "do this—do that" swing tips.

2 Images set the stage for motor responses, i.e. when you imagine something, your muscles are cued up to get the job done.

How imagery works

While you use all your senses to figure out the world, most people have a dominant sense system in which they are most comfortable when they process information and plan responses to their environment.

- If you're a visual person, the image might be aiming the golf ball at a cloud and picturing it dropping out of the cloud next to the pin, or seeing your ball taking off up a ramp with smoke coming out of it, or imaging the ball spouting a parachute as it drops softly onto the green.
- If you're an auditory learner the imagery might be developed using image words such as "syrupy", and "feather", or phrases such as "grip it and rip it", or "finish high and let it fly".
- If you're a feel player, many of your shot-making images will be cued by using a special waggle or taking practice swings that exactly mimic the swing you need to pull out of the shot.

The root images are as varied as the shots you are called on to play, and the ability to match images to the demands of the moment is the creative part of the game. Thus the power of imagery is the defining element in the "golfer as artist." First, you imagine the shot in your mind, then you create the shot with your swing.

When you get to the point where you produce a vivid, multi-sensorial pre-play before each shot, you have added the full *power of imagery* to your catalog of golfing resources. This is a big league addition, and the essential prerequisite of a good player.

How some of the great players describe their imagery

Seve Ballesteros

"In order to gain confidence I must be able to 'see'—clearly visualize mentally—a line all the way from the ball to my actual target, both at the start of the set up...and, equally importantly, at the end of my routine. ...Once everything checks out A-okay, my entire body responds by swinging the club almost reflexively in response to the picture in my mind's eye."

Greg Norman

"...You do want to file the good ones (shots) away for future reference. That way you'll be able to bring them back as part of another reinforcement technique—visualization.

"You envision the ideal shot...in detail. Then you recall successful similar shots from your past and draw confidence from those earlier successes. I can think of favorite shots for every situation I face and I call them forth each time I play."

Jack Nicklaus

"I never hit a shot, even in practice, without having a very sharp, in-focus picture of it in my head. First, I 'see' where I want it to finish. Then the scene quickly changes and I see the ball going there. Then there's a sort of a fade-out, and the next scene shows me making the kind of swing that will turn the previous images into reality."

How do champions play?

Nowhere in the accounts featured here of what the great players think about as they swing do you find any "right elbows or left knees." The point is that it is not a good idea to play the game by conscious manipulation—trying to do something while you swing. This is probably the biggest mistake made by golfers, i.e. they overwhelm the playing of the game by conscious attention to it. To play the game well you need to do just the opposite; you must develop an unconscious competence.

The question is, if they don't play by "don'ts," and they don't play by "do's," how do champions play? The answer is they play by targets. Every shot is a target/player loop or interaction; you are connected to the target by your *senses*.

Champions focus on the target

When you're connected, or plugged into the target, your senses trigger feelings, seeings, rhythms, cadences, etc. and these are translated automatically into motor responses; in other words, your body moves to create the correct distance and direction necessary to send the ball to the target based on the data from your senses.

Play in a flow of go

Your conscious mind/brain is impulsive; it focuses on "doing." It's short term. What's on your mental screen is the momentary goal, your micro-agenda for action. The sentence that best describes your conscious mind/brain is "I'm ready, let's do it."

Your subconscious mind/brain contains all your personal experience. Thus your subconscious is composed of an extensive data base of "silent knowledge." It is contemplative; its focus is evaluation.

Your subconscious mind/brain is long term. It makes value judgments about your capabilities and the appropriateness of your response to the challenges of your environment. It's the arbitrator of motor behavior and the seat of unconscious competence. Your conscious mind/brain needs its approval to get things done effectively. The sentence that best describes your subconscious mind/brain is "Let's wait and evaluate."

When your conscious and subconscious mind are in agreement, all your systems (muscular, neurological, visual etc.) are on the "same page." This total mind/brain/body congruence is expressed as a GO signal.

Getting a GO signal doesn't mean you'll always hit a good shot but it does give you your best chance to play good golf. A constant stream of GO signals is what consistency is all about. A stream of GO is the current that carries you along in the "zone," that super-performance state where you place your golf swing under the control of your unconscious competence, take your hands off the steering wheel and just go along for the ride.

Built in *NO's*

It's wise to remember that many golf course architects practice visual intimidation. They design courses that present to the average player a scary array of bunkers, mounds, water, humpback greens, collection areas and, of course, railway ties. Euphemistically called "challenges," they are arranged to strike visual fear into the golfer's heart. And they do. In the words of course designer Robert Trent Jones Jr. "...the designer may position a tee so that it is exposed to wind and weather in an attempt to distract you and cause you uncertainty. ...Some tees are positioned with the psychological element in mind. For example, some tees are positioned to...create a certain intimidation factor for the golfer. ...Designers love to use this technique to create indecisiveness about your club and shot selection."

How do champions play? *continued*

Science measures the NO/GO signals

Dr. Richard Lonetto conducted recordings of heart rates to determine how golfers perform under stress. There were two different patterns of heartbeats: one associated with good shots and one associated with bad shots. The subjects were 15 tour players and 15 amateurs with handicaps ranging from two to 23.

The good shot pattern

The heart rate profile for good shots corresponded with the subjective reports. When the players were over the ball they reported that their mind was "quiet" with no internal chatter; they felt decisive about their plan, and were completely committed to the shot they had chosen to play. There was an excitement, but it was the anticipation of something good. There were stomach "butterflies" but they were all flying in formation.

Golfers used terms such as solid, balanced, in tune, and in sync, to describe the signals they were getting from their subconscious. These are golfers in conscious-to-subconscious congruence and their feelings are the essence of GO signals.

The bad shot pattern

When the subjects were playing badly, there was also a distinct pattern related to the heart rate which was very different from the "good shot" heart rate. They described being anxious, with lots of negative internal talk; they were not sure they had the right plan and as such weren't committed to the shot. They were anxious about a bad outcome. The butterflies were dive bombing!

These are the messages from your subconscious that poke their way up into your consciousness as NO signals, and if you ignore them and try to play through them, you will never reach your golfing potential no matter how good your swing.

The best way to defeat NO signals is to focus on the characteristics of the target to the exclusion of everything else. Turn your mind outward toward

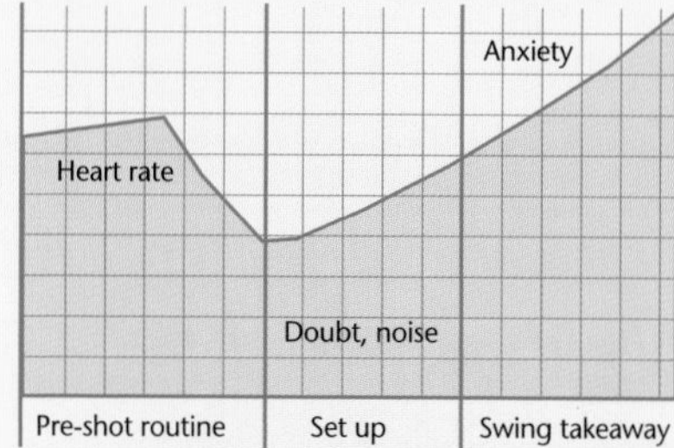

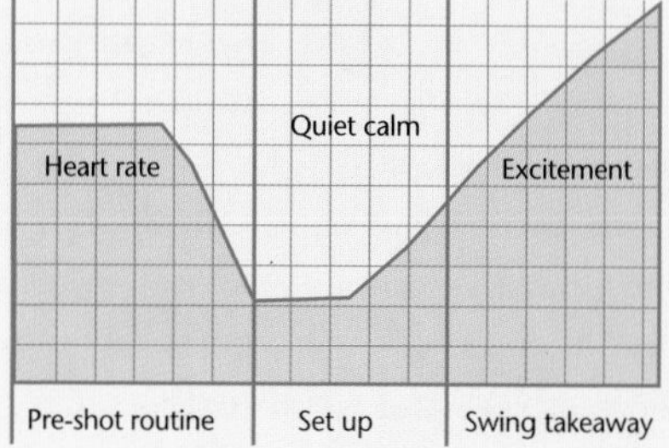

1 The visual intimidation of the water can give you a NO Signal—if you let it.

2 The optical illusion created here by raising the front lip of the greenside bunker is designed to convince the player that there is little or no green on which to land his ball. The result is a NO signal.

3 But when viewed from another perspective there is plenty of green for the player to land his ball on, and, although it may not be apparent, most greens are at least 30 yards from front to back. Our advice is to walk the course from the 18th green to the first tee to gain the correct perspective that will neutralize the architect's optical illusions.

the target, rather than inward toward the consequences. Become a receiving station for the stimuli coming from the target. Occupy your mind with checking out the wind, the distance, the location of the hazards etc.

The key to creating a stream of GO signals—a flow to go—is to gather enough information to pick the shot that best matches your strengths, so that when your subconscious reviews your plan and matches it against your personal strength and weakness profile, it finds everything in order and gives you permission to execute the shot.

A common question is: "Why can I hit it well on the driving range but not on the golf course?" One answer is that there aren't any NO signals on the driving range whereas on the golf course designers have built in a series of NO signals calculated to create a mental havoc that ultimately reverberates down through your pre-shot routine and into your golf swing.

Chapter thirteen

Practice

Goals drive human performance so it's important to practice with a goal. Beating balls with no specific intent is not only wasteful but could be damaging to your game because when it's not engaged in a goal-directed activity, your mind wanders, making it easy for you to tinker yourself right out of a good golf swing. The old saying is true: "Practice does not make perfect, only perfect practise makes perfect." There are four types:

1 Warm up
2 Fundamental building
3 Target orientation
4 "Practice like you play"

Your practice session might contain all four or it might focus on just one, two or three of the different types. The structuring of your program depends on your needs at the time but, whatever the specific content, the key is to have a clear-cut practice plan and to follow that plan.

1 Warm up

All practice sessions, even short game, should begin with a warm up, the purpose of which is to get blood flowing into your golf muscles. A warm up routine also puts you in the mood for what is to come, allowing you to put aside your non-golf concerns so that your mind will be free to focus on your practice session. You should personalize your warm up routine depending on your body profile (strength, flexibility etc.) but, in general, it should include three stages:

- A stretching program that works all the major muscle groups.

Tom Kite, a player known for his long practice sessions, doesn't consider practicing hard work, and perfecting his techniques, including putting, has made him one of the all-time leading money winners in the game.

- A continuous series of dry-run swings without a ball, where your club never stops moving.
- A ball-striking progression, starting with partial swings, that builds up slowly over 10 balls, to full swings.

It's a good idea to get to the course in time to hit a few balls before you play, but take care not

1 At the start of every practice session, loosen your muscles with some stretching exercises. Concentrate on your turning motion, starting out slowly and working up to the normal pace of your swing.

to turn your warm up into a swing overhaul session. Don't search for a swing just before you go to the course. The best way to get ready to play is to do your stretching, then program yourself for solid contact.

There is nothing quite so disheartening as hitting two inches behind the ball on your first warm up swing, so to remove the distraction of the lie of the ball, tee all the balls while you warm up. There is something about the feel of a well-centered hit that programs your brain with good expectations, so your major goal when you warm up is solid contact regardless of where the ball goes. As we have seen in the Inner Game section, with off-centered hits your brain is confused and in doubt, the two centerpieces of NO signals. Square hits, on the other hand, produce a stream of Go signals, just what you want to begin your round.

2 To ensure that your swing is built on a solid foundation much of your practice is focused on grip, stance, posture, correct ball position, aim and alignment. We have found that about 80 percent of all swing errors result from an improper address position, so always use alignment clubs to build a practice station.

2 Fundamental building

All golfers should work on their fundamentals: beginners need to learn them one by one, mid-level players need to integrate them into a coherent whole, and experts need to tweak them now and then to make sure slippage from the perfect form has not occurred. And it's on the practice tee, either on your own or under the direction of a competent golf coach, that you isolate the pieces of your swing for specific attention. But remember that when you're doing "piece work" your evaluation system is not the ball flight but how well you performed the fundamental you're practicing.

Warm up routines *continued*

When you work on target orientation, be sure to go through your pre-shot routine, first stepping behind each ball to look down your target line.

3 Target orientation

The third part of your practice session is called target orientation. In this phase you work on hitting shots to a designated target, focusing only on the target. For each shot, go through your entire pre-shot routine using your power of imagery as the moderator. This is the vital link that helps you take your game from the range to the course.

Switch targets with every shot so your practice will be more realistic. Choose one on the left side of the range, one in the middle and a target on the right side. Change clubs as necessary and don't think about your swing while you target practice. In target practice, the ball flight gives you information and you adjust accordingly. If, while working on target orientation, you begin to hit the ball poorly, abandon target practice and return to fundamental practice. To keep the types of practice distinct in your own mind, remember to announce to yourself that you're switching your practice type.

In general, when you're taking target practice don't be concerned with your swing, and when you're working on your swing don't use a target.

4 Practice like you play

There is a saying that the longest 100 yards in golf is from the practice tee to the first tee. Something seems to happen to your swing along the way so that it's not unusual for a golfer to hit the ball beautifully on the range but poorly on the course. One reason, as we saw in the Inner Game section, is that there are no NO

Next time your round of golf is interrupted by light rain, don't hurry to leave the course. Instead, put on your rain gear and learn to adjust to the bulk of your clothing, wet grips, and the difficult course conditions.

signals on the driving range but there are plenty of them on the course.

Another is that on the course there's a one-ball success rate—you get one try and your brain knows it. Yet most golfers practice a multi-ball success rate by hitting ball after ball with the same club on the driving range. Our suggestion is to devote a major portion of your practice time to gearing up your brain for the one-ball success rate you need to play the game—in other words, practice like you play.

You can actually play a round of golf right there on the practice range, using your imagination to lay out the course, going through your pre-shot routine and hitting the shots required given the situation you have created. Place your bag next to your practice station with your entire complement of clubs therein (avoid bringing just one or two clubs when you're practicing as you play). The hole you're playing should have a specific yardage: it might be an actual hole you've played, one you've seen or heard about, or its outline could be purely your own creation.

A sample hole

Say it's a 400-yard par four that's a slight dogleg to the right. You choose your driver and attempt to hit a fade; you catch it solidly but it drifts just outside the boundaries of your imaginary fairway, coming to rest in the right rough. You have 140 yards left to the green but you have to hit the ball high over the trees that guard the dogleg.

A seven iron does the job and you finish high and let it fly—right over the trees but just short of the green. You're left with a medium trajectory pitch shot of about 20 yards which you hit to four feet and make it for your par. Next is the dogleg right, 540-yard par five with water in the driving area on the right side. Practicing like this is an easy and enjoyable way to get in a quick 18 holes.

From this difficult uphill lie, with his golf ball resting on a thin lie, Corey Pavin needs to make several adjustments to his set up as outlined in the section on Awkward Lies. You can be sure that he knows the necessary adjustments and has spent time practicing from these difficult situations.

Adjusting to the conditions

Learn to adjust to the conditions. Unless there's lightning in the area, the next time your round of golf is interrupted by rain don't be in a hurry to leave the course. Instead, put on your rain gear and tough it out for a few holes, learning to adjust

The Diamond *drill*

It's the architect's job to make our golf exciting, so he prepares a progression of tests for us, some requiring the ball to curve to the left, some to the right and some to fly straight. To develop this skill, use the Diamond Drill.

Tee up your ball and arrange three others in a triangle two feet in front of your ball. The top ball of the triangle should be on the target line with the other two on either side. Your task is to hit three balls per series: one that starts over the right ball and curves back to the target; the second goes directly to the target over the front ball; and the third starts over the left side of the diamond and fades back to the target. When you can do three series in a row without mistakes, you merit the title "shot maker."

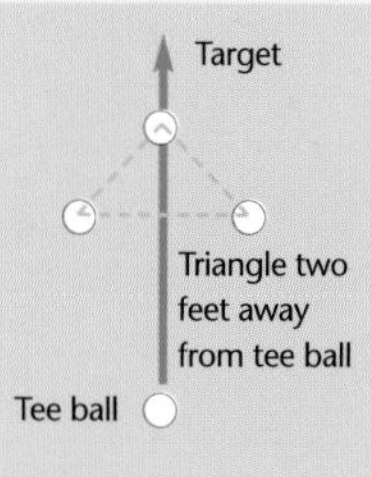

Warm up routines *continued*

to the bulk of your clothing, wet hands and grips, and the difficult course conditions. You don't want your first experience of playing in bad weather to be in a tournament.

Short game practice

A special word on short game practice. As we have said, about 64 percent of all shots taken in a round of golf are from 100 yards and in, so it makes sense that a certain percentage of your practice time should be spent putting, chipping, pitching and in the bunker. However, the percentage of time should vary according to your needs.

A study done by Dr. Lou Riccio shows that for the average amateur the most powerful predictor of score is how many greens in regulation (GIR) the golfer hits. Statistically, each green you hit is equal to two strokes off the average score. For example, if you miss every green in regulation (0 GIR), the average scoring range is in the mid to high nineties. Hit five greens and statistically you'll shoot 85, hit 10 and you're in the mid-seventies.

Play better golf—stat card

	1	2	3	4	5	6	7	8	9	10	11	12	13	14	15	16	17	18	Total
Fairway																			
Green																			
Iron																			
Feet																			
Putts																			
Score																			

Use this form to keep track of your performance on the course. For each hole, check off the fairways and greens that you hit in regulation. Note the iron you chose to hit your approach shot, whether or not your ball actually lands on the green. Once you do hit your ball on the green, note its approximate distance from the hole. At the far right of your stat card, total your stats for 18 holes and you'll quickly see where you need to make improvements. For the irons row, circle the irons that missed the green and practice hitting them more accurately. Circle your three putts and note the distance you began from, then practice lag putting from that distance. Look at your hole by hole score and decide what factors were involved in your good scores and what caused your bad scores. Most of the answers should be right on your stat card.

The next best predictor of score is an index called "Ability To Overcome Distance," and it is related to GIR because you must be able to hit it far enough with accuracy to give you a reasonable chance to hit the green. Putting is surprisingly low for predicting scoring (in fact, it is last). As all golfers know who keep records of their rounds, you can take anywhere between 30 to 40 putts on any given day and shoot a score between 75 to 90 depending on how you drove the ball, how accurate your approach irons were and how close you chipped to the hole after missing the green. Thus, putts per round for the average player is not a good predictor of score. Making a 20-foot putt for an eight saves you one stroke but making an eight on a par four costs you four shots.

The point is that it is how well the various parts of your game fit together that determine how strong your overall game will be. Therefore tailor your practice time allotment to your strength and weakness profile. No matter how good your short game, if your GIR are low, you won't score to your capacity and, conversely, if your long game is strong but you can't get up and down, you need to focus on your short game.

Remember

When you're playing well, you think you'll never play badly again, and when you play badly, you're sure you'll never play well again. Neither is true but if you practice correctly you'll keep your "good" swing longer.

Practice specifics

- Tee all shots.
- Lay down alignment clubs to form your practice station.
- When you've done what you came to do—stop. Limit each session to 45 minutes, then take a break.
- Hydrate your body by drinking plenty of water (12 ounces every hour).
- Have a plan for each session and follow it.
- Keep a journal.
- Don't practice in a cross wind.
- Don't let other golfers distract you (you're there to practice, not to chat).
- If it's not working, go back to square one or leave.
- If you can't do it on your own, go to a good teaching pro.
- Don't listen to the golfer who is two strokes better than you, and definitely don't listen to the one who is two strokes worse.

Mental practice

The 17th hole at TPC Sawgrass, surrounded on all sides by water, is one of the most visually intimidating holes on the PGA Tour. But great players like Greg Norman prepare for challenges like this by mentally playing the hole before they even set foot on the course.

Not all practice is done on the driving range. One of the best ways to work on your game is away from the golf course using a combination of full body relaxation plus imagery, a technique similar to those the Eastern Europeans have used for years in some of their Olympic training programs. You can easily learn to summon a deep state of relaxation and then imagine practicing or playing a round of golf, shot by shot.

This type of mental practice is a great way to stay sharp, especially when the weather keeps you indoors. The first step in this technique (the relaxation part) was popularized by the Harvard heart specialist Herbert Benson. In his best-selling book, *The Relaxation Response,* Benson described the ability of patients to lower their blood pressure by using the same highly effective, but very simple, relaxation procedure that with minor modifications can be adapted to improve your golf game.

1 Find a quiet place where you won't be disturbed. Assume a sitting position with your legs folded in front of you and your spine straight, resting against a support, such as a wall. It helps if you use earplugs because it's easier to isolate the sound of your breathing, a key element of the procedure.

2 Inhale through your nostrils so that your breath fills your stomach. Once your abdominal cavity is filled, continue your breath and fill your

upper chest cavity. This method gives you a full exchange that re-oxygenates your blood and expels harmful carbon dioxide.

Once your body is aerated using this low to high technique (first abdominal, then thoracic), force the air out through your mouth using your stomach muscles. Place your hand on your abdomen to feel it swell as you breathe in and contract as you breathe out. Once you get the rhythm, relax and focus on the sound of your breathing to the exclusion of all else.

3 Continue as in step two until you're in a complete state of relaxation. At first, it might take you 15 minutes or more to elicit the Relaxation Response, but as you become more adept, you can do it in less than a minute.

4 Now it's time to play a little golf. Let's say you need some practice hitting your driver. Imagine yourself addressing the ball. Feel, see and hear everything about the scene: the solidity of your stance, the gracefulness of your backswing, the controlled power of your downswing, the squareness of contact, the flight of the ball and, of course, where your ball comes to rest. The more precise you make your image, the more effective your mental practice becomes. And after you practice, you can play a few holes using your power of mental imagery. Many of golf's greatest players—from Ben Hogan to Jack Nicklaus to Greg Norman—have used mental techniques to maximize their performance.

John Cook and his caddy focus on the task at hand, visualizing the putt breaking into the hole.

Chapter fourteen

Key rules

You can knock a ball around a golf course with no regard for any prescribed procedures or regulations, not counting swings and misses, taking mulligans or do-overs and you can even put down a four when you actually made a seven. However, although this may be some other kind of stick and ball game, it's not golf. If you want to learn to play the game of golf, you need to know not only how to hit the ball but also the rules that define the nature of the game.

Even the awesome power of John Daly is not a solution for every problem. From an impossible lie, it is prudent to take a penalty stroke's relief and play on safely from there.

The rules of the game

Play is governed by a body of rules, approved by the United States Golf Association and The Royal and Ancient Golf Club of St. Andrews, Scotland, and because golf is a game where you, the player, are obliged to act as your own referee, it's well worth taking the time to become familiar with the rules and procedures.

Match and medal

There are two styles of competitive golf: stroke play (also known as medal play) and match play. You'll win at stroke play competition by taking the fewest number of strokes. Match play competitions are decided by the number of holes you win over your opponent. Each hole is a separate contest with the hole either won, lost or halved. A hole is halved or tied when you and your opponent make the same score. The rules and their penalties are often different, depending on whether it's match or medal, and it is a good idea not only to read the rule book from cover to cover at least once a year but also to carry one in your golf bag for easy reference while you play. The following is a general overview of the rules you are most likely to encounter.

Play the ball as it lies

In general, you can't advance your golf ball except by striking it with a club. The ball may be marked and lifted once it reaches the putting surface, and in some other instances, but for the most part you play the ball as it lies. If you accidentally cause your ball to move, it costs you a one-stroke penalty. It also counts as a stroke when you swing and miss unless you move the ball accidentally while preparing to tee off; then it can be replaced without penalty.

Teeing off

According to the rules, the teeing ground is the area inside a rectangle formed by an imaginary straight line connecting the tee markers. The sides are parallel lines from the markers extending to a depth of two club lengths. You can use any club for the measurements. The back boundary of the teeing ground is a line connecting the sides of the rectangle (see below). You can tee

Knowing the boundaries of the teeing ground allows you to maximize your strategy off the tee.

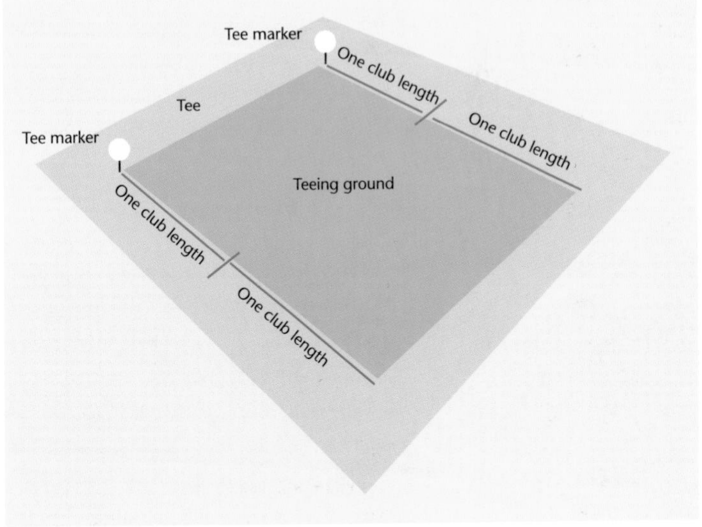

The rules of the game *continued*

your ball anywhere within the confines of this rectangle, including on its boundary lines, but you're not required to stand within this area when you tee off.

Order of play

Who plays first off the first tee is determined by lot. Thereafter the order is determined by honors: the lowest score hits first, the next lowest second and so on. If you make the same score as someone else, the order from the previous tee applies. After teeing off if you're farthest from the hole you hit first.

Once you hit your ball from the teeing ground it's in play and you can't do any thing that improves the lie of your ball or your swing, such as breaking or ripping up anything fixed or growing. You're allowed to remove "loose impediments", such as stones, fallen branches and leaves, except inside the boundaries of a hazard, where you can only remove man-made things, such as paper cups, bottles or cigarette stubs.

Out of bounds

The boundaries of the course are usually marked by white stakes or fences and when your ball comes to rest outside these boundaries it's called "out of bounds" (OB). When you hit your ball out of bounds drop another ball as near as possible to the spot from which you hit it and add a penalty of one stroke.

The easy way to score it is to count the strokes you took with your second ball and add two. For example, on the first tee you hit your tee shot out of bounds, re-tee and make four swings with your second ball before you hole out. That's four plus two for a total of six. It gets a little more complicated when your tee shot is in bounds but you hit your next shot out of bounds. This situation scores as follows: since you must count all swings (except those with a provisional ball) the tally is: one swing off the tee, one swing from the fairway, four swings with the second ball, plus one penalty shot for the out of bounds equals a score of seven. The same procedure is followed for a "ball lost outside a water hazard."

Lost ball

By the way, the definition of a lost ball is one that can't be found or identified as yours, so it is a good idea to place a distinguishing mark with a felt pen on each ball you put into play.

Provisional ball

If you're not sure your ball is OB (the same applies to a lost ball), you should play a provisional ball, until you reach the place where you think your ball should be. If it's OB or lost, your provisional becomes the ball in play and you score as described above, counting all the strokes you make with both balls plus the penalty. If your first ball is not OB, then you must abandon your provisional ball, not counting the strokes you made while playing it.

Hazards

These include permanent water areas, such as ponds, brooks and ditches, whether filled or dry, and the exposed sand or soil in a bunker. When your ball lies in a hazard you can't touch the ground, natural impediments, sand or water with the club until you are making a forward swing.

Regular water hazards

The boundaries of a regular water hazard are defined by yellow stakes. When you hit your ball into a water hazard you have three options:

1 Play it as it lies or take a one-stroke penalty and proceed in one of the following ways.

2 Drop a ball behind the hazard in line with the hole and the point at which the ball last crossed the margin of the hazard.

3 Replay the shot from where your original ball was hit. If it was from the tee, you may re-tee.

Lateral water hazards

These are defined by red stakes. Generally, a lateral hazard runs parallel to the line of the hole. In a lateral hazard you may choose any of the options for a regular water hazard plus two additional ones.

1 You may drop a ball within two club lengths of the point where the ball last crossed the line of the hazard.

2 You may drop a ball within two club lengths on the opposite margin of the hazard at a point that is equidistant from the hole.

Unplayable lies

Occasionally, while you're making your way around the course, your ball finds a place that you can't play from—it might be lodged in a bush or frozen against a tree. You can invoke the unplayable rule anywhere on the course except when your ball is in a water hazard. You then have three options and each one costs you one penalty stroke. You may:

1 Hit a second ball from the same place you hit the first; that's two strokes plus the penalty so you lie three.

2 Drop the ball within two club lengths of the point where the ball lies, but no nearer the hole, and add one penalty stroke so you lie two.

3 Drop a ball directly behind the unplayable lie, in line with the hole, as far back as desired, adding one penalty stroke for a total of two.

Note: If options 2 or 3 are used in a bunker, the ball must remain in the bunker.

When a temporary obstruction interferes with your ability to play your shot, you are entitled to relief under the Rules of Golf.

Bunkers

These are also considered hazards and you must play the ball as it lies without touching your club to the sand when you address the ball in a bunker.

Electrical risers and sprinkler control boxes within the boundaries of the course are generally categorized as immovable man-made obstructions and you are entitled to relief from this situation.

The rules of the game *continued*

Taking relief

- When your ball is unplayable due to a man-made obstruction, such as a sprinkler head, that interferes with your swing or stance, you're entitled to a one club length, no penalty drop.
- When you take relief from an obstruction, ground under repair, casual water or in other instances, the rules require a certain procedure for "dropping" the ball.

1 When taking relief, you should mark the outer limit of the relief area with a tee.

The procedure

1 If you can, always mark your ball's position with a tee before you lift it.

2 Next, mark the spot with a tee that gives you complete relief from the condition for both your stance and swing or, in the case of a hazard, where your ball last crossed the margin of the hazard.

3 From here, measure your club length relief, either one or two depending on the situation, and mark the outer limit of the relief area with a third tee.

4 Stand erect, hold the ball at shoulder height and let it drop. The ball must come to rest within the relief area. If it rolls into a hazard, onto a putting green or outside the relief area, you must re-drop. If it happens a second time, place the ball within the designated area.

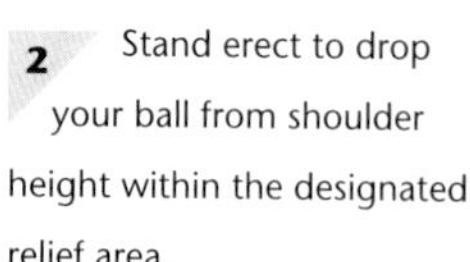

2 Stand erect to drop your ball from shoulder height within the designated relief area.

On the green

On the green you can mark, lift and, if you like, clean your ball. Place something, such as a small coin, directly behind your ball in line with the hole. If your mark interferes with the line of another player's putt, move your mark by using your putter head as a measuring device. Be careful to return your mark to its original position before you putt.

The flag stick

You may ask someone to attend the flag stick and if your ball is on the green the flag stick should be removed to avoid the two-stroke penalty for hitting it. From off the green it's your option to leave the flag stick in the cup because there's no penalty for hitting it in this situation.

On the putting green you can't touch the line of your putt except to repair ball marks, and remove loose impediments. Spike marks on the line of your putt can't be repaired prior to putting, and you can't test the surface of the green by rolling a ball or scraping the surface. If your ball lies on the wrong green, there's no penalty but you must drop the ball off the green.

Summary

These are a few of the rules you need to know to get started. The rules give the game its consistency so that no golfer can have a purely "legalistic" advantage over another. All golfers are treated the same under the rules, being separated at the end of the game only by the difference in skill and good fortune.

Some general thoughts about the rules:

1 If you're taking a drop and there's a penalty stroke assessed, you're entitled to two club lengths relief. When the drop is "free" you get only one club length.

2 Mark your ball with identification and before each stroke check to make sure that it's your ball because there's a penalty for playing the wrong ball.

3 Certain rules are different for match and medal play.

4 Always mark and clean your ball on the green.

5 Before you lift your ball for a drop, always mark its position with a tee and leave it in the ground until after you've made your play.

6 There are three options in a regular water hazard and five in a lateral one.

7 If you're not sure about a rule or procedure, play an alternate ball along with your original and record both scores. Then ask the committee for a ruling after your round.

8 At no time can you drop or place your ball closer to the hole. The phrase that applies is "no nearer the hole."

9 When you call a penalty on yourself, announce it immediately.

10 Don't touch the line of your putt except to fix a ball mark or to remove loose impediments and anything man-made.

11 If your ball sits precariously so that it might move (a penalty) if you soled you club head behind it, hover your club over the ball. By the rules (except in a hazard), you're deemed not to have taken your address position until you sole your club head so there is no penalty.

12 Abide by the basic rule of golf—play your ball from the tee into the hole in accordance with the rules. If a situation isn't covered by the rules, use common sense.

13 The only rule that you can add to the rules is the "rule of fun." Enjoy your time on the course!

Chapter fifteen

Etiquette

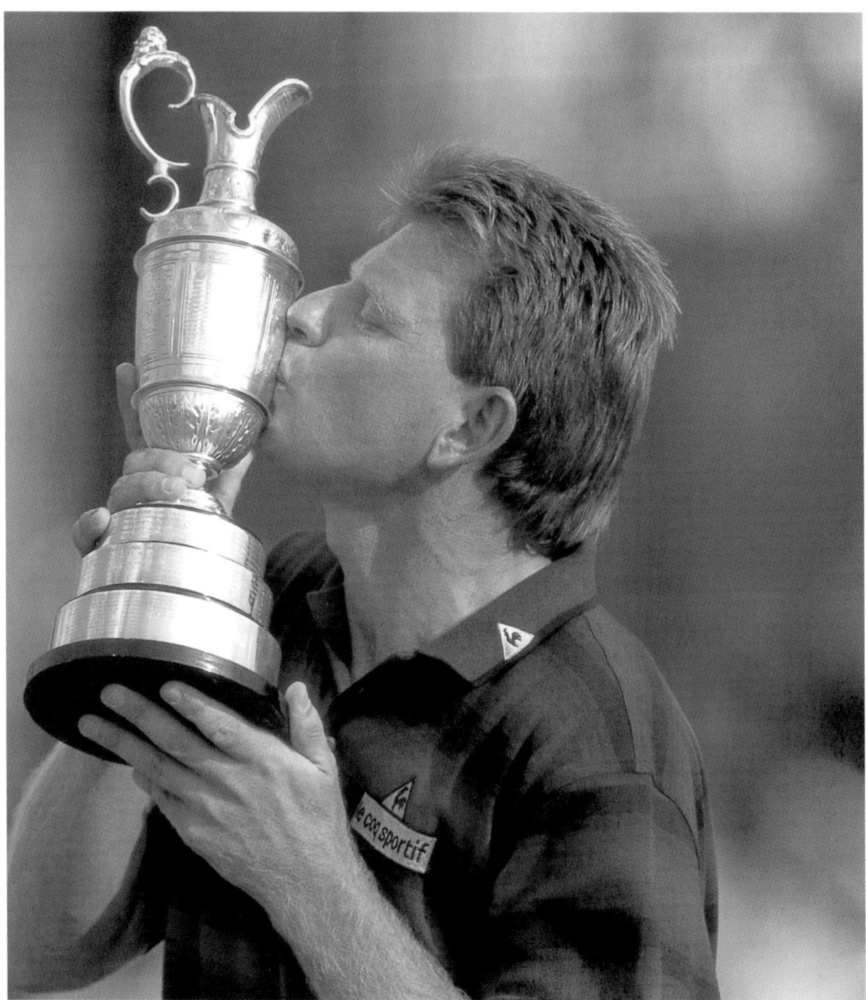

Being awarded the Claret Jug is one of golf's greatest honors and Nick Price receives it graciously and, in good form, gives it a kiss after his 1994 British Open victory.

Golf is a game of refinement played by courteous players whose behavior shows respect for the history of the game, the playing field and their fellow golfers. It is no wonder then that etiquette is the first section in *The Rules of Golf,* a priority driving home the point that certain standards of behavior are an integral part of the game.

Some guidelines

Teeing off

On the teeing ground stand a safe distance to the side of (never directly behind or ahead of) the player who is about to hit. You should stand still so as not to distract their eye. Be complimentary of good performance when they are through making their shot. Poor performance merits either silence or sympathy.

Players in front of you

Hitting into the group in front of you is not only dangerous but very discourteous. A fail-safe way to avoid this is don't hit until all the members of the group ahead have left the area you're hitting to. When it's your turn to play from any position (the tee, the rough, the trees), take a head count to be sure that all the players in front of you have hit their shots and are well on their way to their next shots.

If you hit a ball that looks as if it might strike or land close by to someone, holler "FORE" so that they can take cover.

Distractions and noise

Golf is played on a "quiet" stage so it is very poor form to be the source of distractions of any kind. Jingling change, loud whispering and banging about in the cart while another golfer is trying to play should be avoided.

Avoiding slow play

In the interest of all, play without delay. You don't need to "run" around the course but there's no cause to dawdle either. You can avoid slow play by mentally preparing for your next shot as you're approaching your ball. And you'll be a sought-after playing companion if you limit your practice swings to one.

Lost balls

Golf balls are expensive and a lost ball costs you a penalty stroke, but searching for lost balls is a time-consuming task that can plug up the entire golf course. Under the rules you have five minutes to look but unless you're in a tournament, you'll be a very unpopular golfer if you take more than a minute or two. To cut down on the number of lost balls, everyone in your group should watch each other's shot and mark the landing area.

Golf carts

In riding carts, there's a tendency to cluster around the person who is hitting. Unless your ball is ahead of everyone else's, make sure that you go directly to your ball so you'll be ready to play when it's your turn. If you're dropped off or must leave your cart on the path and walk to your ball, take an array of clubs so that you'll have the right one. Once you've hit your shot get into your cart with your club, waiting to replace it in your bag until the next stop. If you are

Some guidelines *continued*

walking or using a pull cart, replace your club as you walk. It is time consuming to stand there and fiddle with headcovers while the golfers behind you are waiting to play.

Park your cart or position your bag so that when you exit the green you don't have to cross back in front of the green while others are waiting to approach. When you finish the hole, don't linger by the green to calculate your score. Go directly to the next tee and write it down there.

Playing through

For whatever reason, when you've lost your position on the course so that there is a hole open ahead of you, signal to the group behind you, with a wave of your hand, to play through. And when you resume play, speed it up so that you don't lose your position again.

Hazards

These are part of the game so treat them with respect. Enter a bunker from its lowest point closest to your ball. Entering a bunker from its high side can be dangerous and cause damage to the bank. Leave the bunker by the low side but before you go, rake it free of your footprints and divots.

Repairs

Remember that if you're a golfer you're in the repair business. Not only should you rake your bunkers but you should also repair your divots in the fairway and rough, and fix your ball marks on the greens.

Before leaving a bunker, rake smooth your footprints and divot.

Golf carts

Observe the cart rules just as you do the rules of the road. Golf carts should be driven on cart paths as much as possible. Often the courses ask that the 90 degree rule be observed with carts entering from the cart path on a line perpendicular to the ball. In some instances, carts are required to remain on the path to prevent damage to the course. In no case should a golf cart be driven or parked too close to the green.

Golf bags

If you carry your bag or tote it on a pull cart, keep it off the green and the area immediately surrounding it.

Green etiquette

Once on the green check to see if your ball made a hole when it landed. If so, repair it by inserting a tee or similar device into the mark and gently raise it up to level. When removing the flag stick, place, rather than drop, it in an area of the green where it won't interfere with play. Before you leave the green replace the flag stick, being careful not to damage the edge of the hole.

- Don't walk on the line of anyone's putt, including your own, and try not to drag your feet as you walk around on the green. If you do raise some spike marks, be sure to tap them down before you leave the green.

By repairing your ball mark, you will help to keep the putting green in good shape.

On good humor

Nobody likes to play with a whiner or a grumbly grouch. There is no doubt, of course, that golf can raise the primal emotions, creating a roller coaster of feelings ranging from anger to joy. The great Bobby Jones said something to the effect that there are some emotions that one cannot endure with the golf club still in one's hand. This was before dignity replaced impetuousness as the arbiter of his behavior, making his club-throwing period a brief one.

The not so great Guy Lafoon, a mid-forties tour professional, was famous for hurting himself as punishment for a bad shot. He bloodied himself many times, banging his head with his club, and once knocked himself unconscious after missing a critical putt.

While this is extreme behavior exhibited by only a few, for most of us there is a civil expression of the golfing moment. It is best to remember that good humor is always in style.

To understand the different scoring systems involved in golf you'll first need to understand the basics of Par and the Handicap System.

Par

Par is a numerical standard based on the layout of the course. The average course is a total of 18 different holes, each being either a par three, four or five. Par for each hole is based on the amount of strokes required by an expert to negotiate its distance plus two putts on the green. For example, on a par three, the shortest hole, an expert is allotted one shot to get to the green, plus two for putting, for a total of par three. Note, however, that par is a standard based on an expert's performance and therefore the standard is often not reached by the average golfer on a regular basis.

Individual scores are often expressed in relationship to the par for the course. For example, if you were to take 80 strokes on a par 72 course, you would have a score eight strokes over par. If your score is 70 on a par 72, your score could also be expressed as two under par. If, on a par three, you hit your ball short of the green, pitch it onto the green and then two putt, your score would be four or one over par for that hole. This terminology is necessary in understanding the handicap system.

Handicap

Handicap systems were devised to allow players of varying skill levels to compete against one another. Your handicap is related to the number of strokes over par that you average. Although the USGA uses a much more complicated formula to compute handicaps, an easy way to understand the basic idea of handicaps is as follows: if you play 20 rounds of golf and you average a score of 82, i.e. 10 over par, your handicap would be about a 10. If you don't have access to the formal calculating system, you can get an idea of where you stand by using this very general guideline: subtract par from your score to arrive at your handicap.

Forms of play

Stroke play and match play are the two basic scoring systems that apply to both tournament and recreational golf. In the world of amateur golf, a handicap system is often used in conjunction with these forms of play.

Stroke play

You'll win at stroke play when you complete your round in fewer strokes than all your fellow competitors. In a handicapped stroke play competition, your actual score is known as your gross score and from this your handicap is deducted to arrive at your net score. The player with the lowest net score is the winner of a handicapped competition.

The lowest net score is determined as follows. Say the two lowest net scores for this tournament are a 70 and a 73. The player with a net score of 73 was a 10 handicap who had a gross (actual) score of 83 (83 minus 10 = 73). The player with a net score of 70 was a 20 handicap with a gross score of 90. In handicap competition, the player with the lowest net score is the winner; in this example, the 20 handicap would be the winner based on the net score although the actual gross score was higher

Match play

This is a hole-by-hole competition between two individuals or two teams. Each hole is either won, lost or halved (tied). To win at match play you or your team has to win the most holes.

Handicapping match play events is different from the method used in stroke play where you simply deduct the handicap from the actual score. Each hole of a golf course is rated for its difficulty and this rating correlates to handicap. The most difficult hole on the course is known as the number one handicap hole and the system continues for all the holes. Score cards are arranged so that the stroke holes alternate from the front nine to the back nine causing the strokes to be evenly distributed over the course of 18 holes. For example: the # 1 stroke hole is on the front nine and the # 2 stroke hole is on the back nine; the # 3 stroke hole is on the front nine and the # 4 stroke hole is on the back nine.

Before a match play competition, the players compare handicaps. The lower handicap player "gives strokes" to the higher handicap player on the more difficult holes. For example, a 10 playing a 20 handicap would give 10 strokes to the 20 handicap, which is the difference between their handicaps and their skill level. This way they can compete as equals. The strokes are given in this instance on the ten most difficult holes on the course, the five most difficult on the front (handicap numbers 1, 3, 5, 7, 9) and the five most difficult holes on the back (2, 4, 6, 8, 10). Note that these are not hole numbers but the handicap rating that applies to the specific hole. So the 20 handicap could score one stroke higher on these holes and still tie the hole.

Note: stroke play and match play are the official forms of play and the handicap system is a unique and attractive feature of the game of golf which allows golfers of all abilities to play together in a competitive atmosphere.

Chapter sixteen

Learning the game

At the Academy of Golf at PGA National, you will find Director Mike Adams involved in every single school.

There are a number of ways to learn to play better golf. The first step is to choose a model. This involves not only copying the mannerisms and swing motion of an expert player with whom you match up well but also breaking the golf swing down into manageable parts, finding the perfect model for each and then copying that model perfectly until it becomes ingrained as a habit.

One way to do this is to take lessons where the models for every part of the swing are presented to you. Then you take your models and practice them, piece by piece, until you have built a functional swing. Once you've done this, it's time to play the game on the course and that involves knowing how to manage the course and, just as importantly, how to manage yourself.

Please remember, however, that the swing, no matter how well memorized, is still a creative act born out of the conditions of the moment, no two of which are ever the same. Whereas you can reduce the swing to its individual pieces, you cannot reduce the game to a science. It is an art and you are the artist.

Modeling

Human beings are experts at modeling. A young child watches closely how its mother reacts in a certain situation and copies that behavior. If the situation occurs often enough, the behavior becomes a habit. Learning is a combination of nature, the potentials we are born with, and nurture, the experiences that shape our lives. We all have the potential to play better golf; that's the nature part. The question is how well do we organize our experiences so that our learning is efficient and rapid. That's the nurture part, the part that's under your control.

When learning the fundamentals of your set up, even down to the grip, pick a model to try and emulate.

Chuck Hogan in his excellent book, *Learning Golf*, outlines the modeling process as follows: first you pick a model for the piece of the swing you want to learn—it might be the grip, stance or the position of your club at the top of your swing. Then you match that model in every detail. Once you're able to match it perfectly, then you repeat your perfect match until it becomes so ingrained that you can do it automatically every time. At this point it's in your long-term memory and you can now go on to the next "piece."

Learning the game by using a series of precise models as templates is nicely augmented when you choose a golfer as a model. Linda Vollstedt, one of the most successful college coaches in the history of women's golf, encourages her players to use models to enhance what she feels is the common trait among champions: self confidence. Linda says: "You have to practice self confidence, so I have my players think about the qualities associated with being self confident and then practice them." Her first step is to have her players pick "a role model" because, as she points out, "they are going to have to model that behavior." Similarly she advises beginners to pick a model for their swing, but she stresses that when doing so you should realize that everyone is built differently and has a different swing, so pick out a role model who you feel you can be like, i.e. someone with the same body type and a similar level of fitness.

Finding the correct models

Few golfers get to be low handicappers without some form of professional help, especially if they start as adults. You don't need a "perfect" swing but there are a few concepts that you'll need to master if you want to improve. Without these basic concepts, golf really is a difficult game. But with good fundamentals, you can build a repeatable swing that gives you consistent results and sets you on a path toward improvement.

Kinesthetic learners improve most quickly by doing drills that enhance their feel for the golf swing.

Taking lessons

Good teachers have spent years developing the appropriate models for your golf swing, but how do you find these teachers, and how do you "take" a lesson? Remember that your brain learns the imperfect just as well as the perfect, so it's up to you to present it with the perfect.

Since taking a golf lesson is a completely interactive experience you'll give as much as you take in a good learning experience. You'll want to consider not only your instructor's skill level, but also if they are the type of person who shapes the lesson to fit your learning style. It's your lesson and it's up to you to let your instructor know how you want the material presented.

If you learn best by understanding the detailed elements of your golf swing, you'll need an instructor who will teach you details. If you're not a detail person and are more comfortable learning the general concepts in a holistic sense, then that's how your instructor needs to structure your learning experience.

Linda Vollstedt says: "For a novice the most important thing is having the right match with a teacher who can communicate in your learning style. Teaching style is extremely important in the beginning. When you get that right match, where the instructor teaches according to your needs, you learn very quickly."

In other words, it helps to know your own learning style, be it visual, kinesthetic or auditory. If you're primarily a visual learner, find an

Visual learners acquire most of their knowledge of golf through observation.

instructor who will show you your swing on video and can then physically demonstrate the instructions they have for your swing. If you're an auditory learner, find a great communicator who gives precise instructions and explains things clearly. If you're a great athlete who succeeds at most sports without instruction and you don't like complicated thoughts, stick with a teacher who can plug you in to how your swing should feel rather than wasting time with long verbal explanations and detailed video analysis. A good teacher, taking care not to miss the student's dominant learning mode, presents the important material in all three modes so you'll see it, hear it and feel it. It's up to you to direct your instructor in this regard.

To be a good learner, first you should know some things about your own personality and then try to match the instructor to meet your needs. When you find a teacher whose personality and communication style is compatible with your own you'll improve at a much faster rate. Thus, how to find a compatible instructor is an important part of learning to play better golf.

Choosing an instructor

As with any other choice of professional, you'll want to be sure your instructor is well qualified. Verifying their membership of a professional organization is a good place to start. The Professional Golfers Association of America (PGA) and the Ladies Professional Golfers Association (LPGA) are the most highly respected organizations that certify instructors. They each require an apprenticeship for their members and oblige members to continue their education throughout their careers. Like other professional organizations, they have standards their members must fulfill and ethics they must uphold. There are some newer organizations but, so far, their standards are not comparable to the LPGA and PGA. You can call these organizations for verification of your instructor's status or ask them to recommend an instructor in your area.

Male or *female?*

Is it better for women to take lessons from women? Our advice is to choose the most qualified instructor with whom you feel comfortable.

Although it's true that women have, in some cases, been treated as misfits by male instructors, history shows us that many male instructors have dedicated themselves equally to their female students. The late Harvey Pennick, author of the instant instruction classic, *Little Red Book*, not only produced male superstars such as Tom Kite and Ben Crenshaw, but LPGA Hall of Fame members Mickey Wright, Kathy Whitworth and Betsy Rawls.

Interviewing your teacher

Once you verify your teacher's professional status, ask them, or the person scheduling their lessons, about their experience level. How many years have they been giving lessons? How often do they teach? Do they have experience teaching a student at your level? Do they have a certain method of instruction? Do they teach women on a regular basis? Did they plug into your dominant learning mode?

If you're satisfied with your instructor's qualifications, schedule one lesson. Once you get to know your instructor, you may want to schedule a series of lessons. Before you do, though, interview your instructor a little more. Ask what their plan would be for improving your swing over the course of the series. Set some goals together and have the instructor outline the steps you'll take together and what you'll need to do on your own to make significant improvement.

Lesson formats: what to expect

Golf instruction comes in all shapes and sizes. The most common format is an individual lesson, where you and your instructor go to the driving range to work on your swing. The first step should be an interview where your instructor finds out about you and your game. Then you'll be asked to hit a few balls so your instructor can

Repeating the correct motion with the help of a training aid can help you to see and feel how your golf club should work. Your instructor can help you choose the correct training aids and make sure you're using them properly. And, opposite, female students are now treated equally by instructors, both men and women.

get an idea of your natural tendencies: how you hold the club, how you arrange your body in relationship to the ball and target, and the motion of your swing.

Be a good learner

Once your instructor has evaluated your swing, you'll both know what changes you need to make to improve. There may be two or three problems that are causing you trouble but your goal is to prioritize and then fix one problem at a time. While you're working on these changes, don't judge your performance based on where the ball goes, but on whether or not you executed the correct motion. This attention to task performance is the hallmark of a good learner. For example, if you're working on your take away, focus solely on that and your instructor's rating of how well you performed that particular task—don't be controlled by the ball flight. You can see how your brain could get confused. Let's say you make a perfect take away but hit a bad shot. Your teacher says: "Excellent, that's just what we're looking for," evaluating your take away. You say: "What an awful shot." Your brain says: "Well, which is it? Is it good or bad?" And a confused learner is a bad learner.

Learning *golf*

Linda Vollstedt, Head Coach of Arizona State University Women's Golf Team, says, "As the skills and mechanics get to the point where you have a better understanding of the movement of the golf swing (the importance of rhythm, balance and timing), then you can get on the course and learn how to play.

"Learning golf is not just about standing on the driving range hitting balls; you need to get out on the course and learn to play. Many teachers don't teach how to play golf; they teach how to 'swing golf.' But my teaching philosophy is the opposite of most. I feel most teaching should be done on the course, even with beginners. Especially when someone has learned to swing the club and hit the ball. I can teach more in 30 minutes on the course than I can in three days on the driving range."

Choosing an instructor *continued*

Arranging a group lesson for yourself and some friends can be a comfortable way to get started with golf instruction.

Group lessons

Many resorts, clubs and driving ranges offer clinics on different aspects of the game. One session may be dedicated to putting and another to bunker play. Usually the sessions last for an hour or two. Clinics start with a presentation from the teacher on the chosen topic, after which you'll work on these skills. Depending on the size of the group, you'll have varying amounts of individual attention. This is a good way for beginners to get a taste for instruction without a big investment of time or money. It's also a good idea for intermediate golfers who need to brush up on their fundamentals. Group lessons are probably a waste of time for the good player.

If you don't know of a clinic held in your area, it's easy to arrange one for your own group of friends or business associates. First, find out how many participants you'll have and what part of the game your group would like to learn. Then contact your golf professional and arrange the time, date and price structure. Many people find this is an excellent way to get started with instruction, because they are among friends and the program is tailored specifically to their requests.

Short game lessons

Be sure to dedicate at least an equal amount of your lesson to your short game, especially putting, since putting alone accounts for more than 40 percent of your game. If distance isn't your strong suit, a good short game can be a great equalizer. Remember that a two-foot putt counts for just as much on your score card as a 250-yard drive. So either schedule separate short game lessons or divide your lesson time between the full swing and the short game.

Playing lessons

You can have your pro take you on the course for what's known as a playing lesson. The objective here is not to work on your mechanics but your course management skills, and such things as shot selection and how to handle adversity. To do this efficiently, you won't play each shot in succession as you do with your friends, but you'll go to different "situations" and learn to manage your way around the course based on your current golf skills. It is impossible to learn to play golf on a driving range so, once you have some basics, be sure your golf pro takes you on the course and teaches you the essence of the game.

1 If you're serious about lowering your handicap, be sure to dedicate at least an equal portion of your lesson time and practice to your short game skills.

2 When you take playing lessons, you will learn strategy and course management techniques.

Golf schools

When choosing a golf school be sure to check not only the package price but also make a careful inquiry as to the following:

- Find out who actually does the teaching. Is there a "big name" associated with the school? Determine to what extent that person participates in the school you plan to attend.
- Find out the teacher-student ratio; it should be at least four to one if you are going to get enough individual attention.
- Ask about the format of the school: how much time is dedicated to the short game, on-course instruction, etc?
- Ask if your progress is video-taped and if they give you the tape to take home to work from.

The teacher-student ratio is important. Ideally, there should be no more than four pupils in a group.

The Players School at PGA National features course management and mental strategy instruction from Dr. T.J. Tomasi.

Course management and strategy schools

If you are satisfied with your ball striking but need help with your playing ability you can go to a school specifically designed to enhance these skills. Like an in-depth and extended playing lesson, you'll learn how to handle the inner game of golf. Golf is a thinking person's game and schools like this can teach you how to manage your game, your shot selections and your emotions once you get to the course.

Summary

Regardless of what format you choose for instruction, make sure you don't mix yourself up with too many theories. Carefully select your teacher and then stick with that person. Expect to learn golf at a similar rate to which you learned other sports. If this is your first attempt at a sport, relate the learning process to other skills you've acquired: playing the piano, trigonometry, chess, gardening. Regardless of the skill and unless you're a prodigy, learning something new is a process that requires instruction, a dedication to practice and the exercise of your new skills on the course. Golf is no different and you'll get out of it what you put into it.

PGA
National

At the Academy of Golf at PGA National, the Director, Mike Adams, fully participates in every school. The teacher-student ratio, which includes Mike Adams and often Dr. T.J. Tomasi, is generally three to one. The golf school is a comprehensive three-day program, during which students work on all basic elements of the game: full swing, putting, chipping, pitching, side-hill and awkward lies, fairway and green side bunkers, as well as on-course instruction. A mental strategy program for learning and playing is also given. A student's full-swing instruction with Mike Adams is recorded on their take-home video, as is a program for improvement which Mike goes over with them personally.

Chapter seventeen

Course design and strategy

The Champion Course at PGA National is the annual host of the Senior PGA Championship. To beat the "champ," you'll need to conquer its many challenges, such as sand, water, trees, rough and wind.

One of golf's most compelling features is its playing area. Unlike the uniform boundaries of a soccer field or the rigid dimensions of a tennis court, golf courses come in an endless array of shapes and sizes. At their finest, they are truly a work of art, sculpted by the architect and the whims of nature, to offer golfers a field of play unrivaled in any other sport.

A course can be short in distance and tightly bounded by trees and water, or long and open with heavy rough and treacherous greens. Depending on the location, be it seaside, mountainous or desert, each course offers special situations that challenge you to adapt your skills and strategies to the design features built in by the architect. To conquer the inevitable variations you'll face, you need to understand the features that all golf courses have in common.

The concept of par

A championship course features 18 different holes consisting of a mixture of par threes, par fours and par fives, so named for the number of times it takes an expert to hit the ball from the teeing ground into the hole.

Regulation par

Although there are many ways to "make par" the standard is as follows.

- **On par threes,** the shortest distance holes, you'll hit your ball from the tee to the green in one shot.
- **On par fours,** the intermediate distance holes, you'll hit your tee shot to the ideal landing area in the fairway and from there hit your "approach shot" on to the green.
- **On par fives,** the longest holes on the course, you'll hit your tee shot and your second shot to the ideal landing areas in the fairway, then hit

The regulation par for a par four

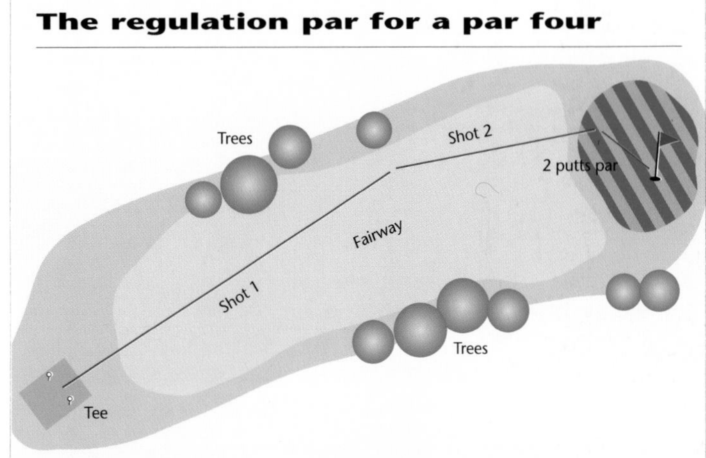

On a par four, you will make a par in "regulation" when you hit your tee shot on to the fairway, your approach shot on to the green, and take two putts to get the ball in the hole.

Design without women in mind

In the past, golf courses were often an intimidating place for women because they were typically designed with two considerations: the professional male golfer and the amateur male golfer. The "ladies" tees were generally an afterthought to course design, if they existed at all. Often these tees were just a few yards ahead of the men's tees, a totally insignificant distance adjustment. When ladies' tees were finally added to courses, they did provide distance adjustments, but often these tees were placed "off to the side" of a hole, forcing women to play from odd angles. Modern-day course architect Rees Jones says: "In the past, forward tees weren't given any thought or as much as they are today so that even if the distance was adjusted, the angle would create an obstacle."

Fortunately, the world of golf course design has changed dramatically and today architects give special attention to the strategic location of each tee box. Even the terminology has changed. Jan Beljan of Fazio Golf Course Designers echoes the modern sentiments of her fellow golf course designers: "We don't call them 'ladies' tees' any more because we have our tees assigned as gender neutral and age neutral." Today's golf courses feature the forward, middle and back tees and golfers are encouraged to choose the tee most appropriate to the distance they hit the ball and their current playing ability. Most newer courses are built with four and five sets of tees so golfers of all levels have an appropriate challenge.

The concept of par *continued*

your approach shot on to the green. Once you reach each green, you are allotted two putts to make your score equal to par.

These examples are what's know as a "regulation par," but since golf is a game where mis-hits are common, even the world's best players sometimes struggle to make par in "regulation," if at all.

The "non-regulation par"

You can still make par even though your tee shot misses the fairway or your approach shot misses the green. For example, on a par four, you might hit your ball into the trees and make an excellent "recovery shot" out of the woods but land just short of the green. From there, you could make what's known as an "up and down" by hitting a difficult pitch shot from heavy rough to within six feet of the hole and sinking the putt. Although not a "regulation" par, you've still made par and on the score card what counts is not "how" but "how many."

At other times, your score will be more than par or "over par" and sometimes when you're firing on all cylinders, you'll get the ball in the hole in fewer strokes than par or "under par."

When you take one stroke more than par, you've made what's known as a bogey; two strokes more than par is a double bogey. Triple and quadruple bogeys follow, and after that nobody's much interested in talking about their score, to say nothing about writing it down. If you take one stroke fewer than par, you've made a birdie, two strokes fewer is an eagle, three fewer is a double eagle. If your tee shot goes in the hole that's known as a hole-in-one. There's nothing normal about a hole-in-one but, when it happens, it's almost always on a par three. In this case you've actually made an eagle (two shots under the par).

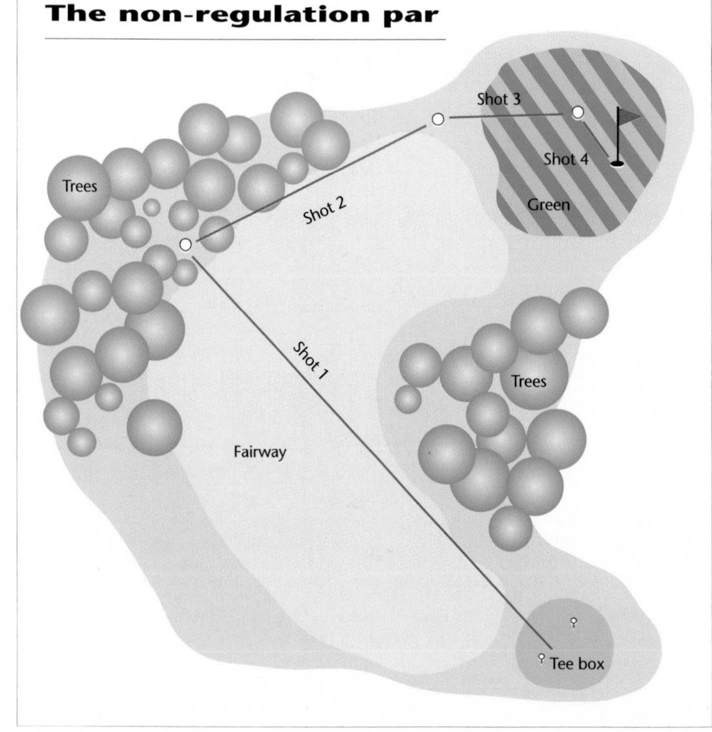

There's an endless variety of ways to make a non-regulation par. In this example, your tee shots finds the trees, your recovery shot is short of the green, your third shot lands close to the hole and you one putt for par.

Guidelines for course management

Rees Jones says: "Definition is important in golf course design today. If an architect designs a hole to help the golfer determine what to do, then the golfer has a better chance of hitting the proper shot and achieving their goal." So when you arrive at the tee box take a few moments to identify the shape of the hole and what the architect had in mind. Each hole has a route from the tee to the green, which is indicated by the fairway, but rarely is it a straight line. Like chess, golf is a game of strategy and you'll need to think a move or two ahead to make a successful plan of attack.

If you're at a new course and the layout of the hole isn't clear from the tee, be sure to look at the map of the hole on your score card or on a placard that's often by the tee box as you drive up to the hole. Or ask one of your playing partners, who knows the course, to give you an idea what's out there.

As you approach the teeing ground, you should check the map of the hole, which is usually located by the back tees.

Know thyself

A successful strategy for playing golf involves knowing your strengths and weaknesses and matching them to the demands of the course. Keep an honest and up-to-date inventory of your current skills and play to your strengths when you get to the course. The more you know about your capabilities the better you can adapt to the demands.

For example, if you're a great fairway wood player but not so great with the driver, use your three or five wood off the tee when you absolutely have to hit the fairway. If you're a good pitcher of the ball but not a good bunker player, you might play short of a deep green side bunker, then pitch your ball safely onto the green. We're not advocating that you be content with your weakness but that you play to your current strengths. Make a note of your weaknesses and then give them special attention on the practice tee. Your strategy is simple: to improve your game, keep your strengths up to date and focus on eliminating your weaknesses.

When faced with difficult bunkers surrounding a green, you should evaluate your current skill level and plan your strategy accordingly.

Guidelines for course management *continued*

Tee shot strategy

Once you've evaluated the layout of the hole, be sure to look at your options from both sides of the tee. Sometimes, a short walk to the other side of the tee gives you a better angle to your target. A good rule of thumb is to tee up on the side of trouble but aim away from it. If you're a slicer of the ball, tee the ball on the right side and aim down the left side of the fairway. If you hit it straight, you're in good shape; if you slice it, the worst result may be that you land in the right rough. The opposite is true for a hooker of the ball.

However, remember that "trouble" is relative to the way you hit the ball. If you tend to mis-hit to the right, you'll be more concerned about the fairway bunker on the right than the large pond on the left. But even if you rarely hit the ball straight, never aim your ball at the trouble and expect it to curve back to safety.

In general, the idea is to always play away from the trouble. What do you do when there's big trouble on both sides of the fairway? Choose a club you know is going to get you on the fairway even if it's a long hole and you have to hit a five iron. You may not be able to reach the green in regulation but you'll avoid penalty strokes, and if you follow your tee shot with a couple of solid shots, you'll be close enough to the green to rely on your short game to keep your score down.

Although the same teeing ground is shown in both pictures, each side of the tee offers a different perspective of the hole. A golfer whose ball flight usually curves from right to left has a better angle from the left side of the tee (1), but from the right side of the tee (2) the margin for error is much smaller due to the proximity of the trees on the right.

Approach shots

On par fours and fives your attempt at hitting your ball on to the green is called your "approach" shot. The first piece of information you need to make a good approach is the yardage to the pin. Most courses have markers or colored disks in the center of the fairway, indicating 100 (red), 150 (white) and 200 (blue) yards to the center of the green. You may also find yardage markings on the cart paths, sprinkler heads or posts on the sides of the fairway that indicate 150 yards. Check to find out how the course is marked and if the yardage is measured to the front or center of the green (it's usually to the center).

Once you have your yardage to the center of the green, locate the pin in relation to that figure. Most greens are at least 30 yards deep so if the pin is in the back of the green, you need to add about 10 yards to your distance; if it's in the front, you need to subtract about 10 yards. Once you know the yardage, take into consideration how conditions, such as wind and elevation, will affect your ball flight.

Most courses feature markers or colored disks in the fairway which indicate your yardage to the green.

Wind

If you're playing in windy conditions, you need to determine exactly how much distance it will effectively add to or subtract from your shot. You can ignore anything less than five miles per hour but if it's blowing more than that, you'll need to adjust your club selection. You won't have a scientific way to measure the strength of the wind, but as a golfer you'll learn to use the measuring devices available to you.

- For example, if your shirt sleeves are fluttering in the breeze and your hair is blowing about, you probably have more than a five-mile-per-hour wind.
- Look at the clouds to see how quickly they're moving, as well as the flagstick to see if it's waving and in what direction.
- If the shot you're planning will get above the tree-tops, pay close attention to the amount and direction in which they are moving.

Once you've made your analysis, adjust your club selection as follows: for every five to ten miles per hour of wind, add one club if you're hitting into the wind, and subtract one if it's behind you.

A side wind is not a helping wind because for most of its journey, your ball is fighting the wind. It's only at its apex when it blows your ball sideways that the wind can be considered helpful. You adjust for a side wind, using about two-thirds of what you would adjust for a head wind of the same speed—for example, a side wind of nine miles per hour is treated as a head wind of six miles per hour.

Lie and elevation

First, you must take your lie into consideration.

- From the rough, if the grass is moving in the same direction as you intend to hit your ball, it causes the ball to jump off the club face so you can figure your ball will travel a greater distance.

Strong *winds*

The key to playing in the wind is to hit the ball solidly. So the old saw, "When it's breezy, swing easy," is a good guide. Since you've already compensated for the wind by adding a club, avoid the temptation to swing "hard" in a head wind. If you do, the chances are that you'll mis-hit your ball and the wind will have an even greater effect. Be confident that you have the right club and make "solid contact" your objective.

In a side wind, most players over-estimate its force and aim off the green expecting the wind to blow it back on. As you learned in Tee Strategy, never aim where a straight shot will get you into trouble, or, in golf lingo, don't "give the green away." You should favor one side or another, but never aim off the green as a compensation for a side wind.

In windy conditions, tee your ball as you normally would and keep your ball position the same. Unless you're an expert player, making variations to your set up often contributes to mis-hits.

Approach shots *continued*

- If the grass is against you, it slows down the club, robbing you of distance, so take one club more.

You should also adjust your club selection depending on how much the green is below or above you. The guideline is that for every 30 feet of elevation, add (uphill) or subtract (downhill) 10 yards.

Pin placement

The location of the pin has a major influence on the type of shot you should play and there are many times during each round where you should not be aiming directly at the flag. Knowing when to attack and when to play safe is the hallmark of a good player.

Tucked pin

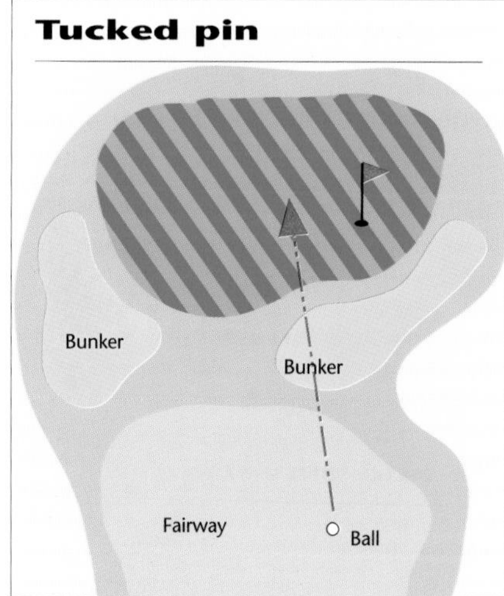

When the pin is "tucked" behind a hazard as shown here, you should always be sure to play to the safe part of the green.

Tucked pins

In golf lingo, a flagstick that is set behind a bunker or a water hazard just a short distance from the edge of the green is said to be "tucked." In this situation, it's difficult to get your ball close to the hole on your approach shot unless you know how to fade and draw the ball on command. Even expert golfers allow some margin for error for these difficult shots. If the pin is tucked left, and you can reliably draw the ball, aim at the center of the green and let the ball curve to the left, close to the pin. This way, if you happen to hit it straight, you're still in the middle of the green.

The cardinal sin in this situation is aiming straight at the flagstick. Unless your shot is perfect,

Front, middle and back pins

When using the red, yellow and green lights method, remember not to confuse this mental strategy with the actual colors of the flags. Many courses feature different flag colors to indicate whether the pin is in the front, middle or back of the green. Each course is different, but often you'll see red flags for front pins, white flags for middle pins and blue flags for back pins. These colors are often chosen because they have a loose correlation to the yardage disks in the fairway and the traditional colors of the tee markers. Thus red indicates short distance, white—medium, and blue—long distance. Before you play, be sure to ask about the color coding and don't confuse it with your red, yellow and green lights strategy.

your margin for error is too small—which is why it's called a "sucker pin." A mis-hit aimed directly at a tucked pin usually winds up in the bunker or rough with very little green between your ball and the hole. This is called "short siding" yourself because you have a short amount of green on which to stop your ball. So when the pin is tucked, the smart player, depending on strengths and weaknesses, aims to the middle or safe side of the green.

Red, yellow and green lights

A good way to identify the type of pin you're dealing with is to label it in your mind by colors.

- Red light = don't go for it.
- Yellow light = proceed with caution.
- Green light = go for it.

Here's how it works. Evaluate the location of the pin based on the conditions. If a pin is protected by two conditions, such as a bunker, with a strong side wind that will blow your ball toward the bunker, then that's definitely a red light pin. If so stop aiming at the flag and select a different part of the green as your target.

When the flagstick is protected by one condition, such as a bunker in this instance, use the "yellow light" strategy.

If the pin is protected by only one condition, such as a bunker, then you can aim closer to it, but proceed with caution by giving yourself about a 10- to 15-foot margin of error on the safe side of the pin (the side the bunker is not on). When there is no trouble surrounding the pin, or the pin's in the middle, go right at this green light situation.

Obviously, pin accessibility depends on your talent level so once again you need to compile a realistic catalogue of your strengths and weaknesses.

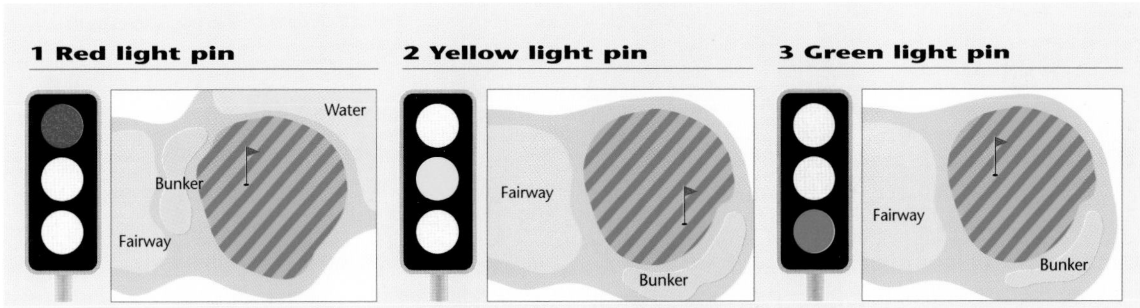

Chapter eighteen

Your first year as a golfer

From the outside, golf seems like a simple game but your first few rounds can prove an arduous task. The golf course offers a variety of situations, each requiring a different club, and sometimes a modified swing and set up. There are rules to learn, customs to follow, and a pace of play to be maintained. All combine to create a good bit of confusion for the beginner. And though this book will clarify some of your confusion, you'll need time to master your skills, learn golf's nuances, and make yourself at home on the course.

For this reason, we offer modifications you can make during your first year as a golfer. Keep in mind, our suggestions are not in accordance with the official Rules of Golf, and are by no means suggested for play when your swing matures. But when you're just learning golf, it's almost impossible to know all the rules, let alone follow them and still complete 18 holes in four hours. Golf is a complex game and, just like anything else you learn, you need to start simple and work toward the more difficult. If you begin your golf career trying to play in strict accordance to the rules it's akin to learning algebra before you learn addition.

Once you're more comfortable on the golf course, begin to familiarize yourself with the Rules of Golf. They are the essence of the game and a true round of golf can be played only when you follow the rules to the letter.

Your first few rounds

If possible, arrange to play your first few rounds with an experienced player. Don't worry that you won't play as well as they do—you're a beginner and therefore you have a perfect excuse. Another choice is to schedule a playing lesson with your golf professional. In both cases, you'll have someone to answer your questions and show you around the course.

A group of beginners

If you decide to play your first round with other new golfers be sure each of you makes some advance preparations. First, make a tee time (an appointment to play) when the course is less crowded so you can take a little longer than more experienced players need. Next, be sure to watch a few rounds of golf on TV. Though your shots probably won't look like those of the pros, observe how they move around the course and the conditions of play subject to commentary. Most importantly, be sure you have taken a lesson or spent some productive time on the practice range before you venture on to the course.

The first tee

This can be a nerve-wracking place even for more experienced players. It's often in view of the clubhouse so you'll feel like a lot of eyes are on you. The common reaction is to rush, but slow down, evaluate your target, and go through your pre-shot routine. This way you'll increase your odds of getting off to a good start. If you badly mis-hit your first shot, a common practice is to take one "mulligan" (another try). Since "mulligans" are not in accordance with the rules, you'd only do so in a casual round if time allows.

Improving your lie

Especially during your first few rounds move your ball from difficult lies (heavy rough, bare ground, difficult stances) to good ones. If someone tells you you're breaking the rules, explain that you're

Especially during your first few rounds, move your ball off difficult lies like this one and play from a good lie.

trying to learn the easier shots before you tackle the more difficult ones and you're not playing for an official score. There is little sense in trying to hit a ball from heavy rough when you're still challenged by a shot from a good lie in the fairway.

Moving along

If you hit a ball that travels only a few yards from the tee, pick it up, bring it out to the fairway where the other members of your group have hit their shots, and play from there. During your first few rounds you may find that several shots in a row go badly. Instead of worrying about holding up the others, just pick up your ball, collect your thoughts, and take another turn after the other members of your group have hit.

Do-over's

Taking a "mulligan" is a common practice on the first tee, but you should avoid this unofficial custom after that for several reasons. First, do-over's are time consuming and, as a beginner, it's likely you'll struggle to keep with the pace of play even without trying the same shot twice. Second, since golf is a social game, it's important to remember the other members of your group are eager for their own turn to play, and hitting a second ball from the same place means your playing companions must wait for you. Third, the superintendent won't appreciate the extra divot you might take. Most courses frown on players who turn the golf course into a practice range. Finally, though we advocate bending the rules to make the game easier during your first year, one of golf's defining features is the fact that you're forced to play your mistakes. Do-over's are contrary to the nature of the game and not a good habit to start.

Safety *Tips*

■ Never position yourself ahead of a player whose turn it is to hit.

■ Engage the parking brake on your cart before you leave it unattended. If you're not sure how to do this ask the cart attendant when you collect your key.

■ When playing out of the woods, remember a misdirected shot could hit a tree and ricochet back at you. Weigh the risks according to your skill level and choose the safest play. Alert your playing partners so they too can be prepared for the possible ricochet effect.

■ If you're looking for your ball along the edge of water, woods, or the desert be careful of snakes. In this situation, it's good to carry a "snake iron" (any iron will do) in case you encounter one of golf's unofficial hazards. Many tropical locations also feature alligators—steer well clear of them.

General rules and safety

On the putting green

Beginners can sometimes be too diligent about the rules they know, especially putting until the ball goes in the hole. But if you've already taken four or five putts, do yourself and your companions a favor and pick up the ball. Before you putt on the next hole, evaluate what went wrong on the last green. If you kept coming up short or long, adjust the force of your stroke accordingly. Limit putts to three and fairway strokes to eight—then carry your ball to the green and putt.

Beginners' par

Par is the standard for an expert golfer. As a beginner you should set appropriate goals for yourself during your first year. One method would be to take the par for a particular hole, say four, and make it your goal to get on the green in that many strokes. Then add the normal two strokes for putting, to arrive at a beginner's par of six for that hole. As you begin to meet your goals, refine them by trying to reach the green in one fewer stroke.

Golf carts

Exercise caution when driving your golf cart, even more so than you would in your car. Sharp turns at full speed can cause a cart to tip over, in which case your open-framed vehicle provides you little or no protection. Be especially careful on steep or wet slopes and avoid injury by keeping your arms and feet safely inside the cart.

Be sure to engage the parking brake on your cart, otherwise it might end up in a hazard.

Novice rules

It's vital to eventually learn and play by the Rules of Golf, so here's a simple description of some you'll deal with most frequently. The official rules are far more complex and the following is only a generalized description.

■ One of golf's most basic rules is to play the ball "as it lies," meaning the rules preclude you from moving your ball except under certain conditions. Once you're on the putting green, the rules allow you to lift and clean your ball after you've marked its location with a coin or similar object.

■ When your ball lands in a bunker, you're not allowed to let your club touch the sand until you actually make your downswing, so hover your club above the sand when you take your address position. If your ball trickles just inside the boundary of a water hazard you're allowed to play it if you can but, as in the bunker, you can't "ground" your club at address.

Usually, when your ball enters a water hazard, you won't have a play. The procedure is to add a stroke penalty to your score and drop your ball according to the rules. To do so, first identify what type of water hazard you've entered. A lateral water hazard is marked by red stakes and is mostly to the side of a hole. Though the rules allow several options, the most common is to drop your ball within two club lengths of where the ball last crossed the margin of the hazard. A regular water hazard is defined by yellow stakes and mostly bisects a hole. You can drop your ball any distance behind this hazard on a line formed by these two points: where your ball last crossed the hazard, and the hole.

When your ball comes to rest "out of bounds," an area literally outside the boundary of the course indicated by white stakes, you're not permitted to play from this location under any circumstances. Under the rules you'd re-play from the place where you originally hit the ball that went out of bounds and add a one stroke penalty to your score. For example, if you hit your tee shot out of bounds, you'd then hit another tee shot and compute your score as follows: one stroke for your first shot, plus a one stroke penalty for going out of bounds and one stroke for your second shot, a total of three strokes to that point. You'd follow the same procedure for a lost ball.

The complete Rules of Golf are available at most golf shops. If not, ask your golf professional how you can acquire a copy. Like golf itself, you'll learn the rules most easily if you first understand the basics and then take time to study the details.

Golf *attire*

Though golf is an athletic event, golf attire is different from what you'd wear to play most other sports. People "dress" for golf and, in addition to specific dress codes, golfers are usually a well polished group. The more exclusive the club or resort, the more likely conservative golf attire is required. For women the standard conservative dress is "Bermuda" or "walking shorts," a golf shirt with a collar, and golf shoes. If you don't have golf shoes substitute shoes with good support, no heel, and a smooth sole. By no means should you walk on a putting or practice green wearing heeled or waffle bottom shoes because they cause damage to the delicate surface. Jeans, short-shorts, and tank tops are prohibited on almost all courses.

The Rules of Golf govern play on all areas of the golf course.

Address (outside a hazard)
Taking your stance and setting the club behind the ball in preparation to swing your golf club.

Albatross
Three strokes under par for a particular hole. Exceedingly rare.

Approach
A shot that you intend to hit on to the putting surface.

Ball-marker
When the ball comes to rest on the putting green, you can mark your ball and clean it if you wish. When you do so, however, you need to place a marker behind the ball before lifting it up.

Ball position
At address your ball rests on an imaginary line extending toward the target, and its position is referred to in relation to your stance. A ball back in your stance means that the ball is further away from the target, more toward your right foot. A ball forward in your stance means the ball is closer to the target, more toward your left foot.

Bare lie
This is when the ball comes to rest on a piece of terrain that has little or no grass beneath it. It is an awkward situation, and restricts the types of shots you can hit from it.

Birdie
This is holing out your ball in one swing less than par.

Bite
A term used when the golfer has managed to get the ball to stop quickly on the green.

Bogey
Holing out your ball in one swing more than par.

- Double bogey: this is two strokes over par.

Carry
This is the distance your ball must fly in the air not counting the roll after it lands.

Chip
A type of shot that is often played around the putting-green. It can be played with virtually any club in the bag, but the back-swing is minimal, as is the follow-through.

Choke down
This is the action of placing your hands further down the grip of your club so that there is an inch or two between the butt end of your club and the top of your hand.

Closed
With regard to the club face, closed means that the face aims to the left of your target. With regard to your body, closed means your shoulders, hips and/or feet are aligned to the right of the target.

Divot
The piece of earth dug up as a player strikes the ball. Etiquette requires that golfers replace divots.

Dogleg
Golf hole that is curved or

angled from right to left or left to right. (Resembling the shape of a dog's hind leg.)

Draw
When struck, the ball curves slightly from right to left.

Drive
When you are playing a par four or par five, the shot off the tee is called a drive.

Eagle
Two strokes under par for a particular hole. This is most commonly achieved on a par five where a long hitter may be able to reach the green in two shots, rather than the allotted three, and one putt for a score of three.

Fade
When struck, the golf ball curves slightly from left to right.

Fairway
Closely mown grass down the central line of play between the tee and the green.

Fat (heavy)
This term is used to describe a mis-hit shot where the club comes into contact with the ground before striking the ball itself.

Flag stick (pin)
A pole with a flag on top of it that sits in the hole on the putting green to indicate the location of the hole. The USGA recommends that it should be at least seven feet high and three-quarters of an inch wide, but in other areas of the world the dimensions vary.

Fore
A warning signal called out by golfers to warn others that they may be in danger of being hit by an errant shot.

Fringe (or apron or collar)
The area immediately surrounding the putting surface, which is often cut at fairway height.

Gimme
The term used for a putt conceded by an opponent without having to hole it because it is so short. There are no gimmes in professional golf or most club competitions.

Green
This is the putting surface.

Handicap
A scoring adjustment based on ability (see scoring systems, page 178).

Hazard
A hazard is any bunker or water hazard. Road, tracks and paths are declared not to be hazards.

Heel
The portion of the club face that is located toward the hosel or neck of the club.

Hole in one
A tee shot that ends up in the hole. Also known as an ace.

Honor
The right to tee off first, due to having the lowest score on the previous hole, or awarded on the first tee on the basis by lot.

Hook
When struck, the golf ball curves severely from right to left.

Hosel
A tubular extension of the club head where the shaft is inserted, located at the heel end of the club.

Iron
This is a club with a thin, flat head, which is usually made of steel, and designed to hit the ball higher, straighter and a shorter distance than woods.

Lag putt
This is a putt that assures that the next putt is easy. A long putt that would be difficult to hole out should be lagged close to the hole for an easy two putt.

Leading edge
The bottom edge of the club face, where the face and the sole meet.

Less club
As in "use less club": choosing a more lofted club that

Glossary

produces less distance, for example, an eight iron instead of a seven iron.

Lie

This has two possible meanings:

- The condition of the ground on which your ball comes to rest.
- The way in which the sole of your golf club rests on the ground. It can lie toe up and therefore be too upright; it can lie with the heel up and therefore be too flat; or it can lie with the sole flush to the ground and the toe slightly up which is the standard.

Links

A golf course constructed on land by, or reclaimed from, the sea.

Lob wedge

This is more lofted than the average sand wedge with about 60 degrees of loft. It is used to hit high shots that produce minimal roll.

Loft

The angle of the club face as measured from the leading edge to the top line of the club when the club is soled flush to the ground.

Mark

Used as a verb, "mark your ball," for example, means to place an object such as a small coin behind your ball to identify its original position once the ball is removed. As a noun it refers to the object used for marking.

Marker

This may refer to the following:

- Tee markers—objects defining the forward boundary of the teeing ground.
- Yardage markers—monuments or markings on the course which indicate yardage from that distance usually to the center of the green.
- In a tournament, a marker is a person who keeps your official score, most often a fellow competitor.

Metal wood

An oxymoron used to describe the materials (metal) that have for the most part replaced the wood in your driving and fairway club heads.

More club

As in "I need more club to reach the green": using a less lofted club that produces greater distance (a five rather than a six iron).

Net

Your net score is the final one when your handicap is taken away from the gross number of shots you have taken.

Open

- With regard to the club face, open means the face aims to the right of your target.
- With regard to the golfer's body, open means your shoulders, hips and/or feet are aligned to the left of the target.

Order of Play

The furthest from the hole

should play first. When golfers are on the teeing-ground, the golfer who shot the lowest score on the previous hole tees off first.

Par

The score an expert is expected to make (see scoring systems, page 178).

Pitch

A high-flying shot, often played with a short-iron, the aim being to land the ball softly on the green.

Pull

The ball travels on a straight line but to the left of the target.

Push

The ball travels on a straight line, but to the right of the target.

Relief

Granted to the golfer when the shot you are trying to play is caused interference by certain impediments, such as casual water, ground under repair and golf car paths. The golfer granted relief is usually entitled to drop the ball not nearer the hole with no penalty.

Reverse C

The follow-through position where the spine is bent backward in a comma-like shape with the head and back foot in alignment.

Rough

The areas on the golf course, usually adjacent to the fair-ways and surrounding the green, which are comprised of thicker, longer grass than found in the fairway. Should be avoided.

Round

A full 18 holes is known as a round of golf.

Sand save

The term given when a golfer lands in a greenside bunker but still saves par by hitting the ball on the green, then making his first putt.

Scratch

When a golfer is "off scratch" it means that he has got his handicap down to zero.

Shank (lateral)

A mis-hit shot where the ball is struck on the heel of the golf club near the neck. It flies severely to the right of the golfer and is also known as the "lateral" or the "pitch out."

Short game

The part of the golf game viewed by the top professionals to be the most important. It incorporates chipping, putting, pitching and bunker play around the green.

Skull (thin)

The term used to describe a mis-hit where the ball is struck more toward the sole of the golf club, bringing about a low, out-of-control running shot.

Sky

A mis-hit ball that is hit very high with drastically reduced distance. It is similar to a pop-up in baseball. It may sometimes leave scratches on the top edge of the driver called "idiot marks."

Slice

The ball curves severely from left to right.

Stroke

Any forward motion of the golf club made with the intention of hitting your ball. You do not have to make contact for a stroke to count. Each stroke counts toward your total score.

Stroke play

The scoring format where the winner is the golfer who has taken the least number of strokes to get around the course.

Tee

A peg, usually made of wood, on which to place your ball from the teeing ground. The teeing ground itself is also referred to as the tee.

Toe

This is the end of the club face opposite the heel.

T

U

V

W

Z